Better Homes and Gardens®

easy
vegetarian

Better Homes and Gardens®

easy
vegetarian

WILEY

John Wiley & Sons, Inc.

John Wiley & Sons, Inc.

Publisher: Natalie Chapman
Associate Publisher: Jessica Goodman
Executive Editor: Anne Ficklen
Production Manager: Michael Olivo
Production Editor: Abby Saul
Cover Design: Suzanne Sunwoo
Art Director: Tai Blanche
Layout: Indianapolis Composition
  Services
Manufacturing Manager: Tom Hyland

Test Kitchen

Our seal assures you that every recipe in *Easy Vegetarian* has been tested in the Better Homes and Gardens® Test Kitchen. This means that each recipe is practical and reliable and meets our high standards of taste appeal. We guarantee your satisfaction with this book for as long as you own it.

This book is printed on acid-free paper.

Published by John Wiley & Sons, Inc., Hoboken, New Jersey

For general information on our other products and services or for technical support, please contact our Customer Care Department within the United States at (877) 762–2974, outside the United States at (317) 572–3993 or fax (317) 572–4002.

Wiley also publishes its books in a variety of electronic formats. Some content that appears in print may not be available in electronic books. For more information about Wiley products, visit our web site at www.wiley.com.

Library of Congress Cataloging-in-Publication Data is available upon request.

ISBN: 978-1-43512-631-2

Printed in China.

10 9 8 7 6 5 4 3 2 1

contents

Appetizers, Snacks,
and Beverages 6

Soups 36

Salads 66

Sandwiches 96

Cheese and Eggs 124

Beans, Rice,
and Grains 152

Pasta 180

Vegetables 208

Metric Information 234

Index 235

appetizers, SNACKS, AND BEVERAGES

Avocado Pesto–Stuffed Tomatoes, *page 8*

avocado PESTO–STUFFED TOMATOES

Prep: 40 minutes
Stand: 30 minutes
Makes: 30 appetizers

- **30 cherry tomatoes (about 1¼ pints)**
- **½ medium avocado, pitted, peeled, and cut up**
- **2 ounces cream cheese, softened**
- **2 tablespoons homemade or purchased basil pesto**
- **1 teaspoon lemon juice**
- **Snipped fresh basil (optional)**

1 Cut a thin slice from the top of each tomato. (If desired, cut a thin slice from bottoms of tomatoes so they stand upright.) With a small spoon or small melon baller, carefully hollow out the tomatoes. Line a baking sheet with paper towels. Invert the tomatoes on the towels. Let stand for 30 minutes to drain.

2 Meanwhile, for filling, in a food processor bowl combine avocado, cream cheese, pesto, and lemon juice. Cover; process until smooth. Spoon filling into a pastry bag fitted with a large plain round or open star tip.

3 Place tomatoes, open sides up, on a serving platter. Pipe filling into the tomato cups. Serve immediately or cover loosely and refrigerate up to 4 hours before serving. Sprinkle with snipped basil before serving.

Nutrition facts per appetizer: 18 cal., 1 g total fat (1 g sat. fat), 2 mg chol., 16 mg sodium, 1 g carb., 0 g dietary fiber, 0 g protein.

eggplant-garlic SPREAD

Prep: 10 minutes
Bake: 45 minutes
Cool: 1½ hours
Oven: 350°F
Makes: 16 servings

1 **medium eggplant (about 1 pound)**

⅓ **cup olive oil**

2 **bulbs garlic, separated into cloves, peeled, and thinly sliced**

2 **tablespoons snipped fresh Italian flat-leaf parsley**

Sweet pepper wedges or low-carb bread, toasted and cut into quarters

1 Preheat oven to 350°F. Halve the eggplant lengthwise; brush all over with olive oil. Grease a shallow baking pan with the remaining olive oil. Place sliced garlic on the cut side of the eggplant halves. Carefully invert eggplant halves onto the prepared pan, tucking garlic slices under the eggplant.

2 Bake for 45 to 60 minutes or until the skin begins to look shriveled. Turn off oven; cool eggplant in oven for 1½ hours.

3 Use a large spatula to carefully transfer eggplant halves and garlic to a serving platter, cut sides up. Sprinkle with parsley. Serve with pepper wedges and/or toasted bread.

Nutrition facts per serving: 53 cal., 5 g total fat (1 g sat. fat), 0 mg chol., 2 mg sodium, 3 g carb., 1 g dietary fiber, 1 g protein.

roasted VEGETABLE DIP

Prep: 20 minutes
Roast: 40 minutes
Oven: 425°F
Makes: 8 (¼-cup) servings

4 medium carrots, cut into
  1-inch pieces

2 large red sweet peppers,
  seeded and cut into
  1-inch pieces

2 medium shallots, halved

3 cloves garlic

1 tablespoon olive oil

½ teaspoon ground black
  pepper

¼ teaspoon salt

2 tablespoons balsamic
  vinegar

1 teaspoon snipped fresh
  rosemary

  Fresh rosemary sprigs
  (optional)

  Assorted crackers or
  assorted vegetable
  dippers (such as broccoli
  florets, cauliflower
  florets, and/or zucchini
  sticks)

1 Preheat oven to 425°F. Line a shallow roasting pan with foil. Place carrots, red sweet peppers, shallots, and garlic in prepared pan. Drizzle with olive oil and sprinkle with black pepper and salt. Cover with foil.

2 Roast for 20 minutes. Uncover and stir vegetables. Roast, uncovered, for 20 to 25 minutes more or until vegetables are tender and lightly browned. Cool slightly on a wire rack.

3 Transfer vegetable mixture to a food processor. Add vinegar and the 1 teaspoon rosemary. Cover and process until smooth. If desired, garnish with rosemary sprigs and serve with crackers and/or vegetable dippers.

Nutrition facts per serving: 49 cal., 2 g total fat (0 g sat. fat), 0 mg chol., 97 mg sodium, 7 g carb., 2 g dietary fiber, 1 g protein.

11

edamame-LEMONGRASS HUMMUS

Start to Finish: 25 minutes
Makes: 10 (¼-cup) servings

2 **scallions**

1 **10-ounce package (2 cups) frozen sweet soybeans (edamame)**

½ **cup fresh Italian flat-leaf parsley sprigs**

½ **cup water**

2 **tablespoons lemon juice**

1 **tablespoon chopped fresh lemongrass or ½ teaspoon finely shredded lemon zest**

1 **tablespoon canola oil**

2 **cloves garlic, quartered**

1 **teaspoon finely chopped fresh ginger, or ¼ teaspoon ground ginger**

¾ **teaspoon salt**

¼ **teaspoon crushed red pepper (optional)**

Assorted vegetable dippers (such as radishes, red sweet pepper strips, Belgian endive leaves, and/or peeled jicama sticks)

1 Thinly slice scallions, keeping green tops separate from white bottoms. Cook edamame according to package directions, except omit salt. Drain; rinse with cold water. Drain again.

2 In food processor, combine white parts of scallions, cooked edamame, parsley, the water, lemon juice, lemon grass, oil, garlic, ginger, salt, and, if using, crushed red pepper. Cover and process until nearly smooth. Stir in scallion tops. Serve with vegetable dippers.

Nutrition facts per serving: 47 cal., 3 g total fat (0 g sat. fat), 0 mg chol., 179 mg sodium, 3 g carb., 2 g dietary fiber, 3 g protein.

Make-Ahead Directions: Prepare as directed, except cover and store in the refrigerator for up to 24 hours.

artichoke-STUFFED NEW POTATOES

Two popular contemporary appetizers—hot artichoke dip and stuffed potato skins—come together in one great nibble. New potatoes and a sprightly gremolata update this dynamic duo.

Prep: 25 minutes
Bake: 20 minutes
Oven: 450°F
Makes: 16 appetizers

16 tiny new potatoes (1½- to 2-inch diameter)

1 tablespoon olive oil

1 14-ounce can artichoke hearts, drained and chopped

½ cup light mayonnaise or salad dressing

¼ cup finely shredded Parmesan cheese

Pinch of ground red pepper

Gremolata*

1 Preheat oven to 450°F. Cut off the top one-third of each potato. Using a melon baller, hollow out the potatoes, leaving ¼-inch shells. Cut a thin slice off the bottom of each potato so it will sit without tipping. (Discard potato trimmings, or cook and use to make potato salad or mashed potatoes.) Lightly brush potatoes all over with oil. Place in a shallow baking pan.

2 For filling, in a medium bowl combine the artichoke hearts, mayonnaise, Parmesan cheese, and ground red pepper. Spoon about 1 tablespoon of the filling into each potato shell.

3 Bake for about 20 minutes or until potatoes are tender and filling is golden brown. Sprinkle the gremolata over the potatoes.

*Gremolata: In a small bowl, combine ¼ cup snipped fresh parsley, 2 tablespoons finely shredded lemon peel, and 2 cloves minced garlic.

Nutrition facts per appetizer: 70 cal., 4 g total fat (1 g sat. fat), 4 mg chol., 144 mg sodium, 7 g carb., 1 g dietary fiber, 2 g protein.

curried CARROT SPREAD

Prep: 20 minutes
Cook: 15 minutes
Chill: 4 hours to 3 days
Makes: 3 cups spread

3 **cups sliced carrots**

¾ **cup chopped onion**

3 **cloves garlic, minced**

2 **tablespoons olive oil or cooking oil**

1 **tablespoon curry powder**

1 **teaspoon ground cumin**

1 **15-ounce can white kidney (cannellini) beans, rinsed and drained**

¾ **teaspoon salt**

Thinly sliced scallions (optional)

Crackers, melba toast, toasted French bread baguette slices, or vegetable dippers

1 In a covered medium saucepan, cook carrots in a small amount of boiling water for about 15 minutes or until very tender. Drain.

2 Meanwhile, in a small skillet, cook onion and garlic in hot oil until tender. Stir in curry powder and cumin. Transfer carrots and onion mixture to a food processor; add white kidney beans and salt. Cover and process until smooth. Transfer to a serving bowl; cover and chill for 4 hours to 3 days.

3 If desired, garnish with scallions. Serve with crackers, melba toast, toasted French bread slices, or vegetable dippers.

Nutrition facts per 2 tablespoons spread: 40 cal., 1 g total fat (0 g sat. fat), 0 mg chol., 84 mg sodium, 6 g carb., 2 g dietary fiber, 2 g protein.

endive-MANGO APPETIZERS

Served individually, endive leaves make stunning appetizers; served as a group, they make an irresistible salad.

Start to Finish: 20 minutes
Makes: about 24 appetizers

1 3-ounce package cream cheese, softened

¼ cup coarsely chopped macadamia nuts

2 to 3 medium heads Belgian endive, separated into individual leaves

1 large mango or papaya, cut into thin strips

1 In a small bowl, combine the cream cheese and macadamia nuts. Spread about 1 teaspoon of the cream cheese mixture onto each endive leaf.

2 Top with the mango strips. Arrange on a serving platter.

Nutrition facts per appetizer: 30 cal., 2 g total fat (1 g sat. fat), 4 mg chol., 11 mg sodium, 2 g carb., 0 g dietary fiber, 0 g protein.

Make-Ahead Directions: Prepare as above through step 1. Loosely cover with plastic wrap; chill for up to 2 hours. Before serving, top with mango strips.

caramelized ONION–BLUE CHEESE DIP

Start to Finish: 35 minutes
Makes: 8 (¼-cup) servings

1 **tablespoon olive oil**

1 **large sweet onion, halved and cut into thin slivers**

8 **ounces cremini mushrooms, chopped**

½ **of an 8-ounce package reduced-fat cream cheese (Neufchâtel), softened**

⅓ **cup crumbled blue cheese**

¼ **cup fat-free milk**

1 **teaspoon snipped fresh thyme or sage**

⅛ **teaspoon salt**

⅛ **teaspoon ground black pepper**

Pear slices, melba toast, and/or whole grain crackers

1 In a large nonstick skillet, heat olive oil over medium heat. Add onion. Cover and cook in hot oil for 10 minutes, stirring occasionally. Uncover and add mushrooms. Cook, uncovered, for 8 to 10 minutes or until mushrooms are tender and onion is golden brown, stirring occasionally.

2 Add cream cheese, blue cheese, milk, thyme, salt, and pepper to onion mixture. Cook and stir over low heat until mixture is melted. Serve warm with pear slices, melba toast, and/or whole grain crackers.

Nutrition facts per serving: 99 cal., 7 g total fat (3 g sat. fat), 15 mg chol., 172 mg sodium, 6 g carb., 1 g dietary fiber, 4 g protein.

swiss AND OLIVE GALETTE

Prep: 25 minutes
Bake: 30 minutes
Oven: 375°F
Makes: 6 to 8 servings

½ of a 15-ounce package
   (1 crust) rolled
   refrigerated unbaked
   pie crust

1 tablespoon olive oil

1 cup finely chopped leeks
   (white part only)

½ cup finely chopped fresh
   fennel

¾ cup coarsely chopped
   kalamata olives

1 tablespoon snipped fresh
   thyme

4 ounces Gruyère cheese,
   shredded (1 cup)

Snipped fresh fennel tops
(optional)

1 Allow pie crust to stand at room temperature according to package directions. Preheat oven to 375°F. Line a large baking sheet with parchment paper. Roll pastry into an 11-inch circle on prepared baking sheet.

2 In a medium skillet, heat olive oil over medium heat. Cook leeks and fennel in hot oil for 5 to 6 minutes or until tender but not brown. Remove from heat. Stir in olives and thyme. Cool slightly.

3 Spread mixture in the center of the pastry, leaving a 1½-inch rim uncovered on the edge. Fold uncovered pasty up over filling. Top with cheese.

4 Bake for 30 to 35 minutes or until pastry is golden. If desired, sprinkle with snipped fennel tops. Cut into wedges and serve warm.

Nutrition facts per serving: 221 cal., 15 g total fat (5 g sat. fat), 18 mg chol., 303 mg sodium, 16 g carb., 1 g dietary fiber, 5 g protein.

Make-Ahead Directions: Prepare as directed through step 3. Cover and chill for up to 24 hours. Continue as directed in step 4.

hummus-and-cucumber
BRUSCHETTA

Prep: 25 minutes
Bake: 10 minutes
Oven: 400°F
Makes: 24 bruschetta

24 ¼-inch slices baguette-
style French bread

Olive oil nonstick cooking
spray

1 tablespoon Italian
seasoning, crushed

½ teaspoon garlic powder

⅔ cup finely chopped
English cucumber

¼ cup low-fat plain yogurt

1 tablespoon lemon juice

1 tablespoon snipped fresh
oregano, or 1 teaspoon
dried oregano, crushed

¾ cup purchased hummus

Snipped fresh oregano
(optional)

1 Preheat oven to 400°F. Arrange baguette slices in a single layer on a large baking sheet. Lightly coat baguette slices with cooking spray. In a small bowl, combine Italian seasoning and garlic powder; sprinkle over baguette slices. Bake for about 10 minutes or until slices are crisp and lightly brown. Cool in pan on wire rack.

2 Meanwhile, in a small bowl combine cucumber, yogurt, lemon juice, and the 1 tablespoon snipped oregano. Spread hummus on top of toasted baguette slices; top with cucumber mixture. If desired, sprinkle with additional snipped oregano.

Nutrition facts per bruschetta: 98 cal., 3 g total fat (0 g sat. fat), 0 mg chol., 170 mg sodium, 15 g carb., 2 g dietary fiber, 3 g protein.

herbed DEVILED EGG BRUSCHETTA

These toasts make lovely dinner appetizers. Or serve alongside a salad as a light lunch for four.

Start to Finish: 45 minutes
Makes: 8 servings

- 4 **eggs**
- 2 **tablespoons snipped fresh chives**
- 1 **tablespoon snipped fresh dill**
- ¼ **cup mayonnaise**
- 1 **tablespoon Dijon-style mustard**
- 4 **slices sandwich bread, toasted**
  Salt and ground black pepper
  Paprika
- 2 **tablespoons chopped baby dill pickles**
- 2 **tablespoons capers**

1 Place eggs in single layer in medium saucepan; add water to cover by 1 inch. Bring to rapid boil (large, rapidly breaking bubbles) over high heat. Cover; remove from heat. Let stand for 15 minutes. Drain; place in bowl of ice water until cool enough to handle. Peel immediately under cool running water.

2 In shallow dish, combine chives and dill. Roll peeled eggs in herbs to coat. Transfer eggs to cutting board; slice. Stir mayonnaise and mustard into remaining herbs.

3 Cut toast diagonally in half; remove crust.

4 To serve, spread each toast triangle with some of the Dijon spread and egg slices. Sprinkle with salt, pepper, and paprika. Serve with chopped baby dill pickles and capers.

Nutrition facts per serving: 123 cal., 8 g total fat (2 g sat. fat), 108 mg chol., 412 mg sodium, 7 g carb., 0 g dietary fiber, 4 g protein.

onion AND OLIVE FOCACCIA

Prep: 30 minutes
Rise: 1 hour 20 minutes
Bake: 25 minutes
Oven: 375°F
Makes: 2 rounds
(24 servings)

3¼ to 3¾ cups bread flour or
all-purpose flour

1 package active dry yeast

1¼ cups warm water (120°F
to 130°F)

1 tablespoon olive oil or
cooking oil

1 teaspoon salt

2 tablespoons olive oil or
cooking oil

1½ cups chopped onions

2 cloves garlic, minced

1 cup sliced pitted black
olives and/or snipped
oil-packed sun-dried
tomatoes, drained

2 tablespoons snipped
fresh rosemary, or
2 teaspoons dried
rosemary, crushed

1 In a large bowl, combine 1¼ cups of the flour and the yeast. Add the warm water, the 1 tablespoon oil, and the salt to the flour mixture. Beat with an electric mixer on low to medium speed for 30 seconds, scraping sides of bowl frequently. Beat on high speed for 3 minutes. Using a wooden spoon, stir in as much of the remaining flour as you can.

2 Turn out dough onto a lightly floured surface. Knead in enough of the remaining flour to make a stiff dough that is smooth and elastic (8 to 10 minutes total). Shape dough into a ball. Place in a lightly greased bowl; turn once to grease surface. Cover and let rise in a warm place until double in size (about 1 hour).

3 Punch down dough. Turn out onto a floured surface. Divide in half. Shape each portion of the dough into a ball. Place on 2 lightly greased baking sheets. Cover; let rest for 10 minutes.

4 Meanwhile, in a medium skillet heat the 2 tablespoons oil over low heat. Add onion and garlic; cover and cook for 3 to 5 minutes or until onion is tender, stirring occasionally. Uncover; cook and stir just until onion begins to brown. Remove from heat. If using olives, stir into onion mixture.

5 Using your hands, flatten each ball to about 10 inches in diameter. With your fingertips, make ½-inch-deep indentations every 2 inches. Spoon onion mixture over dough. Sprinkle with rosemary. Cover and let rise in a warm place for 20 minutes.

6 Meanwhile, preheat oven to 375°F. Bake for about 25 minutes or until golden. If using dried tomatoes, sprinkle over bread for the last 5 minutes of baking. Remove from baking sheet; cool on wire racks.

Nutrition facts per serving: 94 cal., 3 g total fat (0 g sat. fat), 0 mg chol., 147 mg sodium, 15 g carb., 1 g dietary fiber, 3 g protein.

spicy TOFU TRIANGLES

Vegetarians prize tofu as a champion of versatility—it melds perfectly with so many flavors and cooking styles. It's right at home wrapped into wonton skins with intriguing Asian ingredients.

Prep: 50 minutes
Bake: 10 minutes
Oven: 400°F
Makes: 48 appetizers

1 12-ounce package extra-firm, tub-style tofu, chopped

½ cup finely chopped fresh shiitake or button mushrooms

⅓ cup thinly sliced scallions

¼ cup finely chopped canned water chestnuts

2 tablespoons bottled hoisin sauce

2 teaspoons Oriental chili sauce with garlic

1 teaspoon soy sauce

48 wonton wrappers

Nonstick cooking spray

Teriyaki sauce or prepared Chinese-style hot mustard (optional)

1 Preheat oven to 400°F. For filling, in a large bowl combine tofu, mushrooms, scallions, water chestnuts, hoisin sauce, chili sauce, and soy sauce. Spoon about 1 tablespoon of the filling into the center of each wonton wrapper. Brush edges of wrapper with water. Fold one corner of wrapper to opposite corner to form a triangle; press edges to seal.

2 Lightly coat large baking sheets with cooking spray. Place the wonton triangles on prepared baking sheets. Lightly coat the triangles with cooking spray. Bake for about 10 minutes or until triangles are crisp and golden brown. Drain on paper towels. If desired, serve the hot triangles with teriyaki sauce.

Nutrition facts per appetizer: 32 cal., 0 g total fat (0 g sat. fat), 1 mg chol., 67 mg sodium, 6 g carb., 0 g dietary fiber, 1 g protein.

triple-pepper NACHOS

Prep: 25 minutes
Bake: 13 minutes
Oven: 425°F
Makes: 6 servings

5 **7- to 8-inch whole wheat flour tortillas, or 4 ounces baked tortilla chips (about 5 cups)**

Nonstick cooking spray (optional)

1 **15-ounce can black beans, rinsed and drained**

¾ **cup purchased chunky salsa**

1 **cup shredded reduced-fat Colby and Monterey Jack cheese (4 ounces)**

¾ **cup bottled roasted red sweet peppers, drained and cut into strips**

1 **bottled pepperoncini salad pepper, seeded and cut into strips**

2 **to 4 tablespoons bottled sliced pickled jalapeño chile peppers, chopped***

Light dairy sour cream (optional)

Thinly sliced scallions (optional)

Purchased chunky salsa (optional)

① Preheat oven to 425°F. If using whole wheat flour tortillas, lightly coat both sides of each tortilla with nonstick cooking spray. Cut each tortilla into 6 wedges. Place wedges in a single layer on a very large ungreased baking sheet. Bake for 8 to 10 minutes or until lightly browned and crisp, turning once halfway through baking. Tortilla wedges will continue to crisp as they cool.

② Meanwhile, in a medium saucepan combine black beans and the ¾ cup salsa; cook and stir over medium heat just until heated through.

③ On a very large ovenproof platter, arrange tortilla chips one to two layers deep, overlapping slightly. Spoon bean mixture on chips. Sprinkle cheese, roasted red peppers, pepperoncini pepper, and jalapeño peppers over bean mixture on chips.

④ Bake for about 5 minutes or until cheese is melted. Serve nachos immediately. If desired, serve with sour cream topped with scallions and additional salsa.

Nutrition facts per serving: 201 cal., 7 g total fat (3 g sat. fat), 13 mg chol., 838 mg sodium, 24 g carb., 11 g dietary fiber, 15 g protein.

*Tip: Because chile peppers contain volatile oils that can burn your skin and eyes, avoid direct contact with them as much as possible. When working with chile peppers, wear plastic or rubber gloves. If your bare hands do touch the peppers, wash your hands and nails well with soap and warm water.

four-cheese STUFFED MUSHROOMS

Prep: 20 minutes
Bake: 20 minutes
Stand: 10 minutes
Oven: 350°F/450°F
Makes: 24 appetizers

- **24 large fresh mushrooms (1½ to 2 inches in diameter)**
- **1 tablespoon olive oil**
- **8 sun-dried tomatoes (not oil-packed)**
- **Boiling water**
- **1 cup light ricotta cheese**
- **½ cup finely chopped fresh spinach**
- **½ cup shredded Monterey Jack cheese (2 ounces)**
- **3 tablespoons freshly grated Parmesan cheese**
- **1 tablespoon snipped fresh basil**
- **2 cloves garlic, minced**
- **¼ teaspoon salt**
- **¼ teaspoon ground black pepper**
- **½ cup crumbled feta cheese (2 ounces)**
- **Fresh basil leaves (optional)**

1 Preheat oven to 350°F. Remove and discard mushroom stems. Brush mushroom caps with oil. Arrange in a shallow baking pan, stem sides down. Bake for 12 minutes. Drain off any liquid. Increase oven temperature to 450°F.

2 Meanwhile, in a small bowl cover dried tomatoes with boiling water; let stand for 10 minutes. Drain tomatoes, discarding liquid. Coarsely snip tomatoes.

3 In a medium bowl, combine snipped tomatoes, ricotta cheese, spinach, Monterey Jack cheese, Parmesan cheese, snipped basil, garlic, salt, and pepper. Turn mushroom caps stem sides up; fill caps with ricotta mixture. Sprinkle feta cheese over tops.

4 Bake for 8 to 10 minutes or until heated through and lightly browned. If desired, garnish with basil leaves.

Nutrition facts per appetizer: 42 cal., 3 g total fat (1 g sat. fat), 8 mg chol., 105 mg sodium, 2 g carb., 0 g dietary fiber, 3 g protein.

Make-Ahead Directions: Prepare as directed through Step 3. Cover and chill for up to 24 hours. Preheat oven to 450°F. Bake mushrooms for 8 to 10 minutes or until heated through and lightly browned. If desired, garnish with basil leaves.

tofruity SIPPER

With just four nutrient-packed ingredients and one whirl of the blender, you've created the perfect breakfast for busy weekday mornings.

Start to Finish: 10 minutes
Makes: 2 (1½-cup) servings

1½ cups orange juice

½ of a 12.3-ounce package light silken-style tofu, drained

1 medium mango, peeled, pitted, and cut up

1 cup frozen, unsweetened whole strawberries

1 In a blender container, combine orange juice, tofu, mango pieces, and strawberries. Cover and blend until smooth.

2 Pour into tall glasses.

Nutrition facts per serving: 209 cal., 2 g total fat (0 g sat. fat), 0 mg chol., 77 mg sodium, 43 g carb., 4 g dietary fiber, 7 g protein.

apricot ICED TEA

Instead of pouring from a pitcher, you can ladle this drink from a punch bowl with a floating ice ring. To make the ring, place apricot wedges or unsprayed edible flowers in a ring mold, fill with water, and freeze until firm.

Prep: 15 minutes
Stand: 5 minutes to 1 hour
Chill: 4 to 48 hours
Makes: 21 (8-ounce) servings

16 black tea bags

12 cups boiling water

 1 cup loosely packed fresh mint leaves

 6 11.5- to 12-ounce cans apricot nectar

 2 teaspoons vanilla

    Ice cubes

    Fresh apricot wedges (optional)

    Fresh mint sprigs (optional)

1 In a very large heatproof pitcher,* combine tea bags, boiling water, and mint leaves. Let steep for 5 minutes. Remove and discard tea bags and mint. Cover tea; let stand for 1 hour. Stir in apricot nectar and vanilla. Cover and chill for 4 to 48 hours.

2 To serve, fill tall glasses with ice cubes. Pour tea mixture over ice cubes. If desired, garnish with apricot wedges and/or mint sprigs.

Nutrition facts per serving: 55 cal., 0 g total fat (0 g sat. fat), 0 mg chol., 3 mg sodium, 14 g carb., 1 g dietary fiber, 0 g protein.

*Tip: If you do not have a very large heatproof pitcher, halve the recipe and prepare it using a large heatproof pitcher.

cranberry-PINEAPPLE COOLER

Prep: 10 minutes
Chill: 1 hour
Makes: 14 (about
        8-ounce) servings

½ **cup sugar**

½ **cup water**

2 **cups cranberry juice, chilled**

1 **cup orange juice, chilled**

1 **cup unsweetened pineapple juice, chilled**

¾ **cup lemon juice, chilled**

1 **2-liter bottle ginger ale, chilled**

Ice cubes

Fresh cranberries (optional)

Lemon slices (optional)

1 For syrup, in a small saucepan, combine sugar and the water. Cook and stir over medium heat until sugar is dissolved. Transfer to a small bowl or a 1-cup glass measure. Cover and chill for 1 hour.

2 In a large punch bowl, stir together cranberry juice, orange juice, pineapple juice, lemon juice, and chilled syrup. Slowly pour ginger ale down side of bowl; stir gently to mix. Serve over ice cubes. If desired, garnish with cranberries and lemon slices.

Nutrition facts per serving: 118 cal., 0 g total fat (0 g sat. fat), 0 mg chol., 12 mg sodium, 30 g carb., 0 g dietary fiber, 0 g protein.

soups

Caramelized Onion Soup, *page 43*

a to z VEGETABLE SOUP

Thin slices of Parmesan cheese make a scrumptious garnish for this colorful soup featuring a medley of garden vegetables. The hot soup softens the cheese to a delightful consistency.

Start to Finish: 45 minutes
Makes: 4 servings

- 1 tablespoon cooking oil or olive oil
- 2 cups cut-up mixed vegetables, such as sliced small zucchini, carrots, celery, and/or chopped red onions
- 2 14-ounce cans vegetable broth
- 2 cloves garlic, minced
- 1 15-ounce can white kidney (cannellini) or Great Northern beans, rinsed and drained
- ½ cup dried alphabet-shaped pasta or tiny shells
- 1 tablespoon snipped fresh oregano, or 1 teaspoon dried oregano, crushed
- 1 ounce Parmesan cheese, thinly sliced (optional)

1 In a large saucepan heat oil over medium heat. Add mixed vegetables. Cook, uncovered, about 5 minutes or until vegetables are crisp-tender, stirring occasionally.

2 Stir broth and garlic into saucepan. Bring to boiling. Stir in beans, pasta, and dried oregano (if using). Return to boiling; reduce heat. Simmer, covered, about 10 minutes or until pasta is just tender. Stir in fresh oregano (if using).

3 To serve, ladle soup into bowls. If desired, top each serving with Parmesan cheese slices.

Nutrition facts per serving: 166 cal., 5 g total fat (1 g sat. fat), 0 mg chol., 995 mg sodium, 29 g carb., 6 g dietary fiber, 10 g protein.

root VEGGIE SOUP WITH CURRY CROUTONS

For a golden crowning touch, sprinkle the optional croutons onto this first-rate meal-in-a-bowl.

Prep: 25 minutes
Bake: 15 minutes
Cook: 25 minutes
Oven: 350°F
Makes: 4 servings

- 1 **medium fennel bulb (4 to 5 ounces)**
- ¼ **cup chopped onion**
- 1 **clove garlic, minced**
- 2 **teaspoons cooking oil**
- 3 **cups vegetable broth**
- 1 **medium turnip, peeled and cubed (about ¾ cup)**
- 1 **medium potato, peeled and cubed (about ⅔ cup)**
- 1 **medium carrot, sliced (½ cup)**
- ¼ **teaspoon ground white or black pepper**
- 1 **15- or 19-ounce can white kidney (cannellini) beans, rinsed and drained**
- ¼ **cup half-and-half or light cream**
  Curry Croutons* (optional)

1 Cut off and discard upper stalks of fennel, snipping and reserving feathery leaves for garnish. Remove any wilted outer layers of fennel and discard; remove core. Finely chop remaining fennel; set aside.

2 In a large saucepan cook onion and garlic in hot oil over medium heat about 5 minutes or until onion is tender. Carefully add chopped fennel, broth, turnip, potato, carrot, and pepper. Bring to boiling; reduce heat. Simmer, covered, for 25 to 30 minutes or until vegetables are very tender. Cool slightly.

3 Place one-third of the vegetable mixture in a blender container or food processor bowl. Cover and blend or process until smooth. Repeat twice with remaining mixture. Return all of the mixture to saucepan. Stir in beans and half-and-half. Heat through; do not boil. Season to taste with salt.

4 To serve, ladle soup into bowls. If desired, top each serving with Curry Croutons. Garnish with snipped fennel leaves.

*Curry Croutons: In a medium bowl combine 1 tablespoon olive oil and ½ teaspoon curry powder. Tear three ¾-inch slices Italian bread into bite-size pieces. Add the torn bread pieces to the oil mixture; toss until coated. Spread bread pieces in a single layer in a 15x10x1-inch baking pan. Bake in a 350°F oven for 15 to 20 minutes or until croutons begin to brown, stirring once.

Nutrition facts per serving: 282 cal., 10 g total fat (2 g sat. fat), 6 mg chol., 1103 mg sodium, 42 g carb., 16 g dietary fiber, 14 g protein.

cheesy MEXICAN-STYLE VEGETABLE SOUP

Prep: 15 minutes
Cook: 6 to 8 hours (low)
or 3 to 4 hours
(high)
Makes: 5 or 6 servings

2 cups chopped zucchini

¾ cup chopped red or green
sweet pepper (1 medium)

½ cup chopped onion
(1 medium)

1 15-ounce can black beans,
rinsed and drained

1 10-ounce package frozen
whole kernel corn,
thawed

1 14.5-ounce can diced
tomatoes with green
chile peppers

1 16-ounce jar cheddar
cheese pasta sauce

1 cup reduced-sodium
vegetable broth

Coarsely crushed tortilla
chips (optional)

Sliced fresh jalapeño chile
peppers* (optional)

1 In a 3½- to 4-quart slow cooker, place zucchini, sweet pepper, onion, beans, and corn. Pour undrained tomatoes over vegetables and beans. Combine cheese sauce and broth; pour over all.

2 Cover and cook on low-heat setting for 6 to 8 hours or on high-heat setting for 3 to 4 hours. Ladle soup into bowls and top with crushed tortilla chips and jalapeño slices, if desired.

Nutrition facts per serving: 289 cal., 14 g total fat (5 g sat. fat), 35 mg chol., 1381 mg sodium, 36 g carb., 7 g dietary fiber, 12 g protein.

*Tip: Because chile peppers contain volatile oils that can burn your skin and eyes, avoid direct contact with them as much as possible. When working with chile peppers, wear plastic or rubber gloves. If your bare hands do touch the peppers, wash your hands and nails well with soap and warm water.

caramelized ONION SOUP

Sweet onions and shallots are cooked to a luscious golden brown, intensifying their naturally tantalizing goodness.

Prep: 25 minutes
Cook: 30 minutes
Makes: 6 servings

- 3 **pounds sweet onions, such as Vidalia, Walla Walla, or Maui**
- 3 **tablespoons olive oil or butter**
- 12 **medium shallots, halved (about 12 ounces)**
- 4 **cups vegetable broth**
- 2 **tablespoons dry white wine (optional)**
  Salt and ground black pepper
- 6 **½-inch-thick slices sourdough or French bread (about 4 ounces)**
- 6 **ounces Gouda or Edam cheese, thinly sliced**
  Scallion tops (optional)

1 Cut about ½ inch off the tops of three of the whole onions. Peel off the papery outer leaves. Trim the root ends, but leave them intact. Turn one of these onions so it rests on its top. Cut two thin (about ¼-inch) slices from the center of the onion, cutting down from the root end to the onion top. Be careful to keep these slices intact. Repeat with remaining 2 onions to give a total of 6 thin, center-cut onion slices. Set remaining onions aside.

2 In a large skillet, heat 1 tablespoon of the oil. Carefully add the 6 onion slices in a single layer. Cook, uncovered, over medium heat for 3 to 4 minutes or until golden brown. Turn carefully with a wide metal spatula. Cook about 3 minutes more or until golden brown on second side. Carefully remove from skillet and drain on paper towels.

3 Thinly slice remaining onion portions. Halve and cut remaining whole onions into thin slices. You should have 6 to 7 cups onion slices. In a 4- or 4½-quart Dutch oven, heat the remaining 2 tablespoons oil over medium heat. Stir in the sliced onions and halved shallots. Cook, uncovered, for 20 to 25 minutes or until onion is tender, stirring occasionally. Increase heat to medium-high and cook for about 5 minutes or until onions are golden brown, stirring occasionally.

4 Stir broth and wine, if using, into onions in Dutch oven. Heat through. Season to taste with salt and black pepper.

5 Meanwhile, place bread slices on rack of broiler pan. Place under broiler, about 4 inches from the heat, for about 1 minute or until lightly toasted. Turn bread over; top each piece with a slice of cheese. Broil for 1 to 2 minutes or until cheese just begins to melt.

6 To serve, ladle soup into bowls. Top each with a piece of cheese toast; add a caramelized onion slice and, if desired, a green onion top.

Nutrition facts per serving: 333 cal., 13 g total fat (6 g sat. fat), 32 mg chol., 1118 mg sodium, 41 g carb., 4 g dietary fiber, 14 g protein.

roasted GARLIC POTATO SOUP

The potatoes and garlic are roasted before adding them to the soup. Roasting enriches the flavor of the potatoes and mellows the garlic.

Prep: 15 minutes
Bake: 45 minutes
Cook: 30 minutes
Oven: 425°F
Makes: 6 servings

- 6 **medium baking potatoes (about 2 pounds), peeled and cut into 1-inch pieces**
- 2 **tablespoons olive oil**
- ½ **teaspoon ground black pepper**
- 6 **cloves garlic, peeled**
- 1 **medium onion, chopped (½ cup)**
- 3 **cups vegetable broth**
- 1 **cup water**
- 1 **cup whole milk**
   Salt
- 1 **cup thinly sliced Colby, cheddar, or desired cheese (4 ounces)**

1 Preheat oven to 425°F. Place potatoes in a shallow roasting pan. Drizzle with 1 tablespoon of the olive oil. Sprinkle with pepper. Stir to coat.

2 Roast, uncovered, for 25 minutes. Turn potatoes with a metal spatula. Add garlic cloves. Roast for about 20 minutes more or until potatoes are brown. Set aside 1 cup of the roasted potatoes and garlic.

3 In a 3-quart saucepan, heat remaining oil. Cook and stir onion over medium-high heat for 5 minutes. Add remaining roasted potatoes and garlic to onions in saucepan. Stir in broth and water. Bring just to boiling; reduce heat. Simmer, covered, for about 20 minutes or until potatoes are very tender.

4 Place about half of the potato mixture in a blender container or food processor bowl. Cover and blend or process until nearly smooth. Repeat with remaining mixture. Return all of the mixture to saucepan. Stir in milk. Season to taste with salt. Heat through.

5 To serve, ladle soup into bowls. Top each serving with some of the reserved roasted potatoes and sliced cheese.

Nutrition facts per serving: 266 cal., 12 g total fat (5 g sat. fat), 23 mg chol., 561 mg sodium, 28 g carb., 3 g dietary fiber, 11 g protein.

butternut SQUASH SOUP WITH RAVIOLI

Start to Finish: 30 minutes
Makes: 5 side-dish servings

2 pounds butternut squash

2 14.5-ounce cans vegetable broth

½ cup water

⅛ teaspoon cayenne pepper

1 tablespoon margarine or butter

1 9-ounce package refrigerated cheese ravioli

1 tablespoon molasses (optional)

1. Peel squash. Halve lengthwise. Remove seeds and discard. Cut squash into ¾-inch pieces.

2. In a large saucepan, combine squash, broth, water, and cayenne pepper. Cook, covered, over medium heat for 20 minutes or until squash is tender.

3. Transfer one-quarter of the mixture to a blender container. Carefully blend, covered, until smooth. Repeat until all of the mixture is blended.

4. Return blended mixture to large saucepan. Bring just to boiling. Immediately reduce heat. Simmer, uncovered, for 5 minutes. Add the margarine or butter, stirring until just melted.

5. Meanwhile, prepare the ravioli according to package directions. Drain. Ladle hot squash soup into bowls. Divide cooked ravioli among bowls. If desired, drizzle with molasses.

Nutrition facts per serving: 259 cal., 10 g total fat (5 g sat. fat), 52 mg chol., 933 mg sodium, 36 g carb., 2 g dietary fiber, 10 g protein.

Make-Ahead Directions: Prepare soup as directed, except do not add ravioli. Cool soup. Transfer to an airtight container. Store in the refrigerator up to 2 days or label and freeze for up to 2 months. To reheat, transfer frozen soup to a large saucepan. Cook, covered, over medium-low heat for 15 to 20 minutes or until heated through, stirring often. Cook ravioli as directed and serve with soup as directed.

mushroom, NOODLE, AND TOFU SOUP

Japanese udon noodles are similar to spaghetti. Look for them in Asian markets or in the international section of your supermarket.

Start to Finish: 30 minutes
Makes: 6 servings

6 cups vegetable broth

1 10- to 12-ounce package extra-firm tofu, drained and cut into ½-inch cubes

1 tablespoon soy sauce

1 tablespoon toasted sesame oil

6 ounces sliced fresh shiitake or button mushrooms (about 2¼ cups)

1 tablespoon grated fresh ginger

1 clove garlic, minced

1 tablespoon cooking oil

1 16-ounce package frozen sugar snap stir-fry vegetables

2 ounces dried udon noodles or spaghetti, broken

1 tablespoon snipped fresh cilantro

1 In a large saucepan, bring the broth to boiling. Meanwhile, in a medium bowl gently stir together tofu cubes, soy sauce, and sesame oil; set aside.

2 In a medium saucepan, cook the mushrooms, ginger, and garlic in hot oil over medium-high heat for 4 minutes. Add to the hot broth.

3 Stir the frozen vegetables and udon noodles into the hot broth mixture. Bring to boiling; reduce heat. Simmer, covered, for 10 to 12 minutes or until vegetables and noodles are tender, stirring once or twice. Gently stir in the tofu mixture and the cilantro; heat through.

Nutrition facts per serving: 175 cal., 9 g total fat (1 g sat. fat), 0 mg chol., 1193 mg sodium, 17 g carb., 2 g dietary fiber, 10 g protein.

savory BEAN AND SPINACH SOUP

Prep: 15 minutes
Cook: 5 to 7 hours (low)
or 2½ to 3½ hours
(high)
Makes: 6 servings

3 **14-ounce cans vegetable broth**

1 **15-ounce can tomato puree**

1 **15-ounce can white or Great Northern beans, rinsed and drained**

½ **cup converted rice**

½ **cup finely chopped onion**

2 **cloves garlic, minced**

1 **teaspoon dried basil, crushed**

¼ **teaspoon salt**

¼ **teaspoon ground black pepper**

8 **cups coarsely chopped fresh spinach or kale leaves**

Finely shredded Parmesan cheese

① In a 3½- or 4-quart slow cooker, combine broth, tomato puree, beans, rice, onion, garlic, basil, salt, and pepper.

② Cover; cook on low-heat setting for 5 to 7 hours or on high-heat setting for 2½ to 3½ hours.

③ Stir spinach into soup. Serve with Parmesan cheese.

Nutrition facts per serving: 150 cal., 3 g total fat (1 g sat. fat), 4 mg chol., 1137 mg sodium, 31 g carb., 8 g dietary fiber, 9 g protein.

greek MINESTRONE WITH FETA

Prep: 15 minutes
Cook: 15 minutes
Makes: 4 servings

2 cloves garlic, minced

1 tablespoon extra-virgin olive oil

2 cups stemmed and sliced fresh shiitake mushrooms

3 14-ounce cans vegetable broth

1 15-ounce can cannellini beans, rinsed and drained

½ cup dried orzo

1½ cups quartered cherry tomatoes

¼ cup small fresh oregano leaves

½ cup feta cheese, crumbled

Ground black pepper

1 tablespoon olive oil

1 In a 4-quart Dutch oven, cook garlic in hot oil for 15 seconds. Add mushrooms; cook, stirring frequently, until mushrooms are tender. Stir in vegetable broth and beans; bring to boiling. Add orzo; return to boil. Reduce heat and simmer, covered, for 15 minutes or until orzo is tender.

2 Stir in cherry tomatoes and 3 tablespoons of the oregano; heat through. Sprinkle with remaining oregano, feta, and pepper. Drizzle with olive oil.

Nutrition facts per serving: 312 cal., 11 g total fat (3 g sat. fat), 13 mg chol., 1497 mg sodium, 48 g carb., 8 g dietary fiber, 14 g protein.

white bean AND
CUMIN CHILI

Prep: 20 minutes
Cook: 9 to 10 hours (low)
or 4½ to 5 hours
(high)
Makes: 4 servings

1 **cup chopped onion
(1 large)**

3 **cloves garlic, minced**

2 **14.5-ounce cans
tomatoes, cut up**

1 **12-ounce can beer or
nonalcoholic beer**

1 **chipotle chile pepper in
adobo sauce, chopped**

1 **tablespoon cumin seed,
toasted***

1 **teaspoon sugar**

½ **teaspoon salt**

2 **19-ounce cans cannellini
(white kidney) beans,
rinsed and drained**

1½ **cups peeled, seeded, and
coarsely chopped
Golden Nugget or acorn
squash (about 12 ounces)**

½ **cup sour cream**

2 **tablespoons lime juice**

1 **tablespoon snipped fresh
chives**

Lime wedges (optional)

1 In a 3½ or 4-quart slow cooker, combine onion, garlic, undrained tomatoes, beer, chipotle pepper, cumin, sugar, and salt. Stir in beans and squash.

2 Cover and cook on low-heat setting for 9 to 10 hours or on high-heat setting for 4½ to 5 hours. Meanwhile, combine sour cream, lime juice, and chives; cover and chill until ready to serve.

3 To serve, ladle chili into bowls. Top with sour cream mixture. If desired, garnish with lime wedges.

Nutrition facts per serving: 365 cal., 15 g total fat (5 g sat. fat), 13 mg chol., 995 mg sodium, 52 g carb., 13 g dietary fiber, 17 g protein.

*Tip: To toast cumin seed, place seeds in a dry skillet over low heat. Cook for about 8 minutes or until fragrant, stirring frequently. Remove from heat; allow to cool before grinding in a spice grinder or with a mortar and pestle.

vegetable CHILI
WITH CHEESE TOPPING

A cheddar-chive cream cheese topping adds a soothing counterpoint to this zesty chili.

Prep: 20 minutes
Cook: 45 minutes
Makes: 5 servings

1¼ **cups finely chopped zucchini**

¾ **cup finely chopped carrot**

2 **tablespoons sliced scallion**

2 **cloves garlic, minced**

2 **15-ounce cans hot-style chili beans in chili sauce, undrained**

2 **14.5-ounce cans diced tomatoes, undrained**

1 **tablespoon unsweetened cocoa powder**

1 **teaspoon chili powder**

1 **teaspoon ground cumin**

1 **teaspoon bottled hot pepper sauce (optional)**

¼ **teaspoon dried oregano, crushed**

½ **of an 8-ounce tub cream cheese with chive and onion (½ cup)**

2 **tablespoons milk**

½ **cup shredded cheddar cheese (2 ounces)**

Scallion strips (optional)

1 Lightly coat a large saucepan with cooking spray. Add zucchini, carrot, chopped scallion, and garlic to saucepan. Cook over medium heat for 2 minutes. Add chili beans, tomatoes, cocoa powder, chili powder, cumin, hot pepper sauce (if desired), and oregano. Bring to boiling; reduce heat. Simmer, uncovered, over low heat for about 40 minutes or until desired consistency, stirring occasionally.

2 Meanwhile, for cheese topping, in a small bowl stir together cream cheese and milk until smooth. Stir in cheddar cheese. Ladle chili into bowls. Spoon a little cheese topping onto each serving of chili. If desired, garnish with scallion strips.

Nutrition facts per serving: 328 cal., 13 g total fat (7 g sat. fat), 32 mg chol., 1132 mg sodium, 41 g carb., 11 g dietary fiber, 14 g protein.

harvest CHILI

Prep: 20 minutes
Cook: 36 minutes
Makes: 12 cups

2 **tablespoons olive oil**

1 **large onion, peeled and chopped**

1½ **teaspoons ground cumin**

1 **teaspoon chipotle chile powder (or more if desired)**

2 **28-ounce cans whole tomatoes in puree**

1 **medium cauliflower, cut into florets (about 4 cups)**

2 **medium sweet potatoes (about 1 pound), peeled and cut into ½-inch cubes**

4 **large carrots, peeled and cut into ¼-inch coins**

1 **large green sweet pepper, cored, seeded, and cut into ½-inch dice**

½ **teaspoon salt**

1 **15-ounce can Mexican chili beans**

Sliced scallions, for garnish

Cooked brown rice (optional)

1 Heat olive oil in a large pot over medium-high heat. Add onion and cook for 5 minutes, stirring occasionally. Stir in cumin and chile powder; cook for 1 minute. Stir in tomatoes, breaking up with a spoon.

2 Stir in cauliflower, sweet potatoes, carrots, green pepper, and salt. Cover and bring to a boil. Reduce heat and simmer, covered, for 25 minutes. Stir occasionally. Add chili beans and simmer for 5 minutes or until vegetables are fork-tender.

3 Garnish with scallions and serve with brown rice, if desired.

Nutrition facts per cup: 123 cal., 3 g total fat (0 g sat. fat), 0 mg chol., 502 mg sodium, 20 g carb., 5 g dietary fiber, 4 g protein.

vegetarian GUMBO

Okra and gumbo are a perfect culinary marriage. Okra makes this stew taste special and also helps to thicken it.

Prep: 10 minutes
Cook: 6 to 8 hours (low)
or 3 to 4 hours
(high)
Makes: 6 servings

2 **15-ounce cans black beans, rinsed and drained**

1 **28-ounce can diced tomatoes, undrained**

1 **16-ounce package frozen sweet pepper stir-fry vegetables**

2 **cups frozen cut okra**

2 **to 3 teaspoons Cajun seasoning**

3 **cups hot cooked white or brown rice (optional)**

Chopped scallions (optional)

1 In a 3½- to 4½-quart slow cooker, combine beans, tomatoes, frozen stir-fry vegetables, frozen okra, and Cajun seasoning.

2 Cover and cook on low-heat setting for 6 to 8 hours or on high-heat setting for 3 to 4 hours. If desired, serve over hot cooked rice and sprinkle with scallions.

Nutrition facts per serving: 153 cal., 0 g total fat (0 g sat. fat), 0 mg chol., 639 mg sodium, 31 g carb., 10 g dietary fiber, 12 g protein.

bean AND POTATO CHOWDER

This creamy, warming chowder is just what you want to eat on a cold night. If you don't have Italian seasoning, use ½ teaspoon each of dried oregano and dried basil.

Start to Finish: 20 minutes
Makes: 4 servings

1   **20-ounce package refrigerated diced potatoes with onions**

1   **14-ounce can vegetable broth**

⅓   **cup all-purpose flour**

1   **cup shredded Swiss cheese (4 ounces)**

3   **cups milk**

1   **teaspoon dried Italian seasoning, crushed**

1   **15-ounce can navy beans, rinsed and drained**

    Salt and ground black pepper

    Bottled roasted red sweet pepper (optional)

    Snipped fresh Italian flat-leaf parsley (optional)

8   **slices toasted Italian bread with shredded Swiss cheese (optional)**

① In a 4-quart Dutch oven, combine potatoes and vegetable broth. Cover and bring to boiling; reduce heat. Simmer, covered, for 4 minutes.

② In a large bowl, toss together flour and cheese until cheese is coated. Gradually stir in milk until combined. Add cheese mixture and Italian seasoning to potato mixture in Dutch oven. Cook and stir over medium heat until thickened and bubbly. Stir in beans; cook and stir for 1 minute more. Season to taste with salt and pepper. If desired, top servings with roasted pepper and parsley and serve with toasted, cheese-topped bread.

Nutrition facts per serving: 494 cal., 12 g total fat (7 g sat. fat), 41 mg chol., 1344 mg sodium, 70 g carb., 9 g dietary fiber, 25 g protein.

cheesy POTATO AND CAULIFLOWER CHOWDER

The rye bread is a snappy complement for the rich, nutty, buttery flavor of the Jarlsberg cheese.

Prep: 20 minutes
Cook: 10 minutes
Oven: 350°F
Makes: 6 servings

- 1 **large onion, chopped (1 cup)**
- 2 **tablespoons butter**
- 4 **cups vegetable broth**
- 2 **cups diced, peeled Yukon gold or white potatoes**
- 2½ **cups cauliflower florets**
- 1 **cup half-and-half, light cream, or milk**
- 2 **tablespoons all-purpose flour**
- 2½ **cups shredded Jarlsberg cheese (10 ounces)**
- 3 **slices slices dark rye or pumpernickel bread, halved crosswise (optional)**
- ½ **cup shredded Jarlsberg cheese (2 ounces; optional)**
- 2 **tablespoons snipped fresh Italian flat-leaf parsley (optional)**

1. In a large saucepan or Dutch oven, cook onion in hot butter over medium heat until tender. Carefully add broth and potatoes. Bring to boiling; reduce heat. Simmer, covered, for 6 minutes. Add cauliflower. Return to boiling; reduce heat. Simmer, covered, for 4 to 6 minutes more or until vegetables are tender.

2. In a bowl, whisk half-and-half into flour until smooth; add to the soup mixture. Cook and stir until mixture is thickened and bubbly. Reduce heat to low. Stir in the 2½ cups cheese until melted. Do not allow the mixture to boil.

3. Meanwhile, if using bread, preheat oven to 350°F. Trim crusts from bread. Place the halved bread slices on a baking sheet. Bake for about 3 minutes or until crisp on top. Turn slices over. Sprinkle with the ½ cup cheese and the parsley. Bake for about 5 minutes more or until cheese melts.

4. Ladle soup into bowls. If desired, float a piece of cheese-topped bread in each bowl of soup.

Nutrition facts per serving: 267 cal., 17 g total fat (12 g sat. fat), 58 mg chol., 682 mg sodium, 14 g carb., 2 g dietary fiber, 15 g protein.

jalapeño CORN CHOWDER

Prep: 15 minutes
Cook: 5 minutes
Makes: 4 servings

3 cups frozen whole kernel corn

1 14-ounce can vegetable broth

⅔ cup dried small pasta (such as ditalini or tiny shell macaroni)

1 cup milk, half-and-half, or light cream

¼ cup bottled roasted red sweet peppers, drained and chopped

1 or 2 fresh jalapeño chile peppers, seeded and finely chopped*

½ cup shredded cheddar cheese (optional)

1 In a blender or food processor, combine half of the corn and the broth. Cover and blend or process until nearly smooth.

2 In a large saucepan, combine the broth mixture and the remaining corn; bring to a boil. Add pasta. Reduce heat; simmer, uncovered, for 5 to 7 minutes or until pasta is tender. Stir in milk, roasted sweet peppers, and jalapeño peppers; heat through. Ladle soup into bowls. If desired, sprinkle with cheese.

Nutrition facts per serving: 219 cal., 2 g total fat (1 g sat. fat), 5 mg chol., 419 mg sodium, 45 g carb., 3 g dietary fiber, 8 g protein.

***Tip:** Because chile peppers contain volatile oils that can burn your skin and eyes, avoid direct contact with them as much as possible. When working with chile peppers, wear plastic or rubber gloves. If your bare hands do touch the peppers, wash your hands and nails well with soap and warm water.

provençal VEGETABLE STEW

Experience a bit of France with this stew's fresh veggies, beans, herbs, and spices.

Prep: 25 minutes
Bake: 6 minutes
Cook: 8 to 10 hours (low) or
      4 to 5 hours (high)
Oven: 400°F
Makes: 4 servings

- 2 baby eggplants or
  1 very small eggplant
  (about 8 ounces)
- 1 large zucchini, quartered
  lengthwise and cut into
  ½-inch slices
- 1 large yellow summer squash,
  quartered lengthwise and
  cut into ½-inch slices
- 1 15- to 19-ounce can cannellini
  (white kidney) or Great
  Northern beans, rinsed and
  drained
- 1 large tomato, chopped
- 2 teaspoons bottled minced
  garlic (4 cloves)
- ¼ teaspoon dried rosemary or
  thyme, crushed
- ¼ teaspoon ground black pepper
- 1 tablespoon snipped fresh
  basil, or 1 teaspoon dried
  basil, crushed
- 1½ cups low-sodium tomato juice
- 1 tablespoon white or regular
  balsamic vinegar
- 4 ½-inch slices baguette-style
  French bread
- 2 teaspoons olive oil
- 3 tablespoons finely shredded
  pecorino or Parmesan cheese

1 If desired, peel eggplant. Cut eggplant into ¾-inch pieces (you should have about 3 cups).

2 In 3½- or 4-quart slow cooker, combine eggplant, zucchini, yellow squash, cannellini beans, tomato, garlic, rosemary, pepper, and dried basil, if using. Add tomato juice.

3 Cover and cook on low-heat setting for 8 to 10 hours or on high-heat setting for 4 to 5 hours. Stir in fresh basil, if using, and balsamic vinegar.

4 Meanwhile, for croutons, preheat oven to 400°F. Lightly brush bread slices with olive oil. Sprinkle with 1 tablespoon of the cheese. Place bread slices on baking sheet. Bake for 6 to 8 minutes or until toasted.

5 To serve, ladle stew into bowls. Top with croutons and sprinkle with remaining cheese.

Nutrition facts per serving: 227 cal., 5 g total fat (1 g sat. fat), 4 mg chol., 424 mg sodium, 41 g carb., 10 g dietary fiber, 12 g protein.

pumpkin, CHICKPEA, AND RED LENTIL STEW

Prep: 25 minutes
Cook: 8 to 10 hours (low)
or 4 to 5 hours
(high)
Makes: 6 servings

- **1 pound pie pumpkin or winter squash, peeled, seeded, and cut into 1-inch cubes**
- **1 15-ounce can chickpeas (garbanzo beans), rinsed and drained**
- **3 medium carrots, sliced ½ inch thick**
- **1 cup chopped onion (1 large)**
- **1 cup red lentils, rinsed and drained**
- **2 tablespoons tomato paste**
- **1 tablespoon grated fresh ginger**
- **1 tablespoon lime juice**
- **1 teaspoon ground cumin**
- **¼ teaspoon salt**
- **¼ teaspoon ground turmeric**
- **¼ teaspoon ground black pepper**
- **4 cups vegetable broth**
- **¼ cup chopped peanuts**
- **2 tablespoons chopped fresh cilantro**
- **Nonfat plain yogurt (optional)**

1 In a 3½- to 4-quart slow cooker, combine pumpkin, chickpeas, carrots, onion, lentils, tomato paste, ginger, lime juice, cumin, salt, turmeric, and pepper. Pour broth over all in cooker.

2 Cover and cook on low-heat setting for 8 to 10 hours or on high-heat setting for 4 to 5 hours. Top each serving with peanuts, cilantro, and, if desired, yogurt.

Nutrition facts per serving: 275 cal., 4 g total fat (1 g sat. fat), 2 mg chol., 1027 mg sodium, 46 g carb., 10 g dietary fiber, 14 g protein.

black BEAN AND BROWN RICE STEW

Prep: 15 minutes
Cook: 45 minutes
Makes: 6 servings

1 cup chopped onion

1 cup chopped red sweet pepper

½ cup sliced celery

8 cloves garlic, minced

1 tablespoon olive oil

2 14-ounce cans vegetable broth

2 14-ounce cans black beans, rinsed and drained

3 cups water

1 cup uncooked long grain brown rice

1 teaspoon dried basil, crushed

1 teaspoon dried thyme, crushed

⅛ teaspoon ground black pepper

⅛ teaspoon cayenne pepper

Bottled hot pepper sauce (optional)

1 In a 4- to 6-quart Dutch oven, cook and stir onion, sweet pepper, celery, and garlic in hot oil for about 5 minutes or until onion is tender.

2 Stir broth, black beans, water, rice, basil, thyme, black pepper, and cayenne into Dutch oven. Bring to boiling; reduce heat. Simmer, covered, for about 40 minutes or until rice is tender. If desired, serve with hot pepper sauce.

Nutrition facts per serving: 257 cal., 4 g total fat (1 g sat. fat), 0 mg chol., 881 mg sodium, 50 g carb., 9 g dietary fiber, 12 g protein.

salads

Mesclun Salad with Roasted Pears and Walnuts, *page 68*

mesclun SALAD WITH ROASTED PEARS AND WALNUTS

Start to Finish: 40 minutes
Oven: 350°F
Makes: 2 servings

1 **medium pear, halved and cored**

3 **tablespoons balsamic vinegar**

2 **tablespoons water**

⅓ **cup broken walnuts**

3 **tablespoons extra-virgin olive oil**

1 **tablespoon balsamic vinegar**

½ **shallot or scallion, finely chopped**

½ **clove garlic, minced**

¼ **teaspoon salt**

⅛ **teaspoon ground black pepper**

6 **cups mesclun (assorted baby greens), or one 6-ounce package ready-to-eat spring mix lettuces**

① Preheat oven to 350°F. Place pear halves, cut side down, in an 8x8x2-inch baking pan. Add the 3 tablespoons vinegar and 2 tablespoons water. Cover and bake for 15 to 25 minutes or until tender (baking time depends on ripeness of pears). Remove from oven; set pan on wire rack and uncover; let pears cool in liquid. When cool, lift pears from liquid; discard liquid. Place pears on a cutting board. Slice pears lengthwise from bottom up to, but not through, stem end; set aside.

② Meanwhile, place walnuts on a baking sheet. Bake for 6 to 8 minutes or until light golden. Cool.

③ Stir together olive oil, the 1 tablespoon vinegar, shallot, garlic, salt, and pepper in a large bowl. Add greens; toss to coat. Arrange greens on salad plates. Sprinkle with nuts. Fan a pear half atop each salad.

Nutrition facts per serving: 412 cal., 33 g total fat (4 g sat. fat), 0 mg chol., 289 mg sodium, 28 g carb., 5 g dietary fiber, 5 g protein.

fontina AND MELON SALAD

Start to Finish: 30 minutes
Makes: 4 main-dish
servings

1½ **cups dried large bow-tie**
 pasta (about 6 ounces)

2 **cups cantaloupe and/or**
 honeydew melon chunks

1 **cup cubed fontina or**
 Swiss cheese (4 ounces)

⅓ **cup bottled nonfat poppy**
 seed salad dressing

1 **to 2 tablespoons snipped**
 fresh mint

2 **cups watercress, stems**
 removed

 Cantaloupe slices
 (optional)

1 Cook pasta according to package directions. Drain in colander; rinse with cold water. Drain.

2 Toss together pasta, cantaloupe, and cheese in a large bowl. Combine salad dressing and mint; pour over pasta mixture, tossing gently to coat. Serve immediately or cover and chill for up to 24 hours.

3 To serve, stir watercress into pasta mixture. If desired, garnish with cantaloupe slices.

Nutrition facts per serving: 219 cal., 10 g total fat (6 g sat. fat), 37 mg chol., 355 mg sodium, 23 g carb., 1 g dietary fiber, 10 g protein.

apricot-spinach SALAD

Prep: 25 minutes
Chill: 2 to 24 hours
Makes: 4 servings

- 1 **15-ounce can black beans, rinsed and drained**
- ½ **cup snipped dried apricots**
- 1 **cup red, orange, and/or yellow sweet pepper strips**
- 1 **scallion, thinly sliced**
- 1 **tablespoon snipped fresh cilantro**
- 1 **clove garlic, minced**
- ¼ **cup apricot nectar**
- 2 **tablespoons salad oil**
- 2 **tablespoons rice vinegar**
- 1 **teaspoon reduced-sodium soy sauce**
- 1 **teaspoon grated fresh ginger, or ¼ teaspoon ground ginger**
- 4 **cups shredded fresh spinach**
  Very thin strips scallion* (optional)

1 In a medium bowl, combine black beans, apricots, sweet pepper, 1 scallion, the cilantro, and garlic. In a screw-top jar, combine apricot nectar, oil, rice vinegar, soy sauce, and ginger. Cover and shake well. Pour over bean mixture; toss gently to coat. Cover and chill for 2 to 24 hours.

2 To serve, arrange spinach in a salad bowl. Top with black bean mixture. If desired, garnish with additional scallion.

Nutrition facts per serving: 211 cal., 7 g total fat (1 g sat. fat), 0 mg chol., 336 mg sodium, 33 g carb., 8 g dietary fiber, 9 g protein.

*Tip: To make the scallion curl, soak the thin strips in ice water for 30 to 60 minutes; drain and arrange on salad.

egg salad–stuffed
TOMATOES

Start to Finish: 25 minutes
Makes: 4 servings

6 eggs

6 roma tomatoes

⅓ of a seedless cucumber, chopped (about ¾ cup)

¼ of a red onion, chopped (about ¼ cup)

⅓ cup mayonnaise

1 tablespoon Dijon-style mustard

½ teaspoon salt

½ teaspoon ground black pepper

1 bunch watercress, trimmed

1 In a medium saucepan, cover eggs with water. Bring to a boil over high heat. Remove from heat; cover and let stand for 12 minutes. Drain, rinse, peel, and chop cooked eggs.

2 Meanwhile, halve tomatoes lengthwise and remove seeds. In a bowl, combine cucumber, onion, mayonnaise, mustard, salt and pepper. Fold in chopped egg.

3 Divide watercress among plates. Top each with 3 tomato halves; spoon on egg salad. Drizzle with any remaining dressing.

Nutrition facts per serving: 276 cal., 22 g total fat (5 g sat. fat), 324 mg chol., 610 mg sodium, 8 g carb., 2 g dietary fiber, 12 g protein.

roasted VEGETABLES OVER SALAD GREENS

Prep: 20 minutes
Roast: 40 minutes
Oven: 375°F
Makes: 6 servings

12 **ounces baby beets, or 3 medium beets**

12 **ounces tiny new potatoes, halved**

4 **ounces pearl onions, peeled**

¼ **cup olive oil**

6 **cloves garlic, minced**

1 **tablespoon snipped fresh rosemary or basil, or 1 teaspoon dried rosemary or basil, crushed**

½ **teaspoon salt**

½ **teaspoon coarsely ground black pepper**

2 **tablespoons balsamic vinegar**

1 **tablespoon snipped fresh chives**

1 **tablespoon water**

6 **cups torn Boston or Bibb lettuce**

1 Preheat oven to 375°F. Scrub beets; cut off root and stem ends. (If using medium beets, peel and cut into 1-inch pieces.) In a 13x9x2-inch baking pan, combine the beets, potatoes, and onions.

2 In a small bowl, combine 2 tablespoons of the oil, the garlic, rosemary, salt, and black pepper. Drizzle over vegetables; toss gently to coat. Roast, covered, for 30 minutes. Roast, uncovered, for 10 to 20 minutes more or until vegetables are tender. Cool vegetables to room temperature. Drain, reserving pan drippings.

3 For dressing, in a screw-top jar combine the reserved pan drippings, the remaining 2 tablespoons oil, the balsamic vinegar, chives, and water. Cover and shake well.

4 Divide the lettuce among salad plates. Arrange the roasted vegetables on top of lettuce; drizzle with dressing.

Nutrition facts per serving: 172 cal., 9 g total fat (1 g sat. fat), 0 mg chol., 245 mg sodium, 20 g carb., 3 g dietary fiber, 3 g protein.

three-bread SALAD

Start to Finish: 25 minutes
Makes: 6 servings

**Dried Yellow Tomato
  Vinaigrette***

6   **cups mixed salad greens**

2   **1-inch-thick slices crusty
    sourdough bread, cut
    into irregular pieces**

1   **8-inch whole wheat pita
    bread round, cut into
    12 wedges**

2   **slices pumpernickel
    bread, torn into pieces**

1   **small sweet onion, very
    thinly sliced and
    separated into rings**

1   **cup yellow and/or red
    pear tomatoes
    or cherry tomatoes**

2   **ounces shaved dry
    Monterey Jack cheese
    or other hard grating
    cheese**

1 Prepare Dried Yellow Tomato Vinaigrette. Transfer to a storage container. Cover and chill.

2 In a large salad bowl, combine mixed greens, sourdough pieces, pita wedges, torn pumpernickel, sliced onion, and tomatoes. Drizzle with the Dried Yellow Tomato Vinaigrette; toss gently to coat. Top with cheese.

***Dried Yellow Tomato Vinaigrette:** Place ¼ cup snipped sun-dried yellow or red tomatoes (not oil-packed) in a small bowl. Add 1 cup boiling water; cover and let stand for 10 minutes. Drain tomatoes, reserving ½ cup of the liquid. In a blender container or food processor bowl, combine tomatoes and their reserved liquid; ¼ cup red wine vinegar; 1 tablespoon Dijon-style mustard; 2 teaspoons snipped fresh thyme or ½ teaspoon dried thyme, crushed; ¼ teaspoon salt; and ⅛ teaspoon coarsely ground black pepper. Cover and blend or process until nearly smooth. Gradually add ⅓ cup olive oil, processing until combined and slightly thickened.

Nutrition facts per serving: 269 cal., 16 g total fat (4 g sat. fat), 7 mg chol., 599 mg sodium, 24 g carb., 3 g dietary fiber, 9 g protein.

layered SOUTHWESTERN SALAD WITH TORTILLA STRIPS

Prep: 15 minutes
Bake: 15 minutes
Makes: 6 servings

2   6-inch corn tortillas
    Nonstick cooking spray
½   cup light sour cream
¼   cup snipped fresh cilantro
2   tablespoons fat-free milk
1   teaspoon olive oil
1   large clove garlic, minced
½   teaspoon chili powder
½   teaspoon finely shredded
    lime zest
¼   teaspoon salt
¼   teaspoon ground black
    pepper
6   cups torn romaine lettuce
4   roma tomatoes, chopped
    (2 cups)
1   15-ounce can black beans,
    rinsed and drained
1   cup fresh corn kernels*
½   cup shredded reduced-fat
    cheddar cheese (2
    ounces)
1   avocado, pitted, peeled,
    and chopped
    Snipped fresh cilantro
    (optional)

① Preheat oven to 350°F. Cut tortillas into ½-inch-wide strips; place in a 15x10x1-inch baking pan. Coat tortillas lightly with cooking spray. Bake for 15 to 18 minutes or just until crisp, stirring once. Cool on wire rack.

② For dressing, in a small bowl stir together sour cream, the ¼ cup cilantro, the milk, oil, garlic, chili power, lime zest, salt, and pepper.

③ Place lettuce in a large glass serving bowl. Top with tomatoes, beans, corn, cheese, and avocado. Add dressing and sprinkle with tortilla strips. If desired, garnish with additional cilantro.

Nutrition facts per serving: 227 cal., 11 g total fat (3 g sat. fat), 12 mg chol., 386 mg sodium, 29 g carb., 9 g dietary fiber, 11 g protein.

*Tip: It isn't necessary to cook the corn. However, for a roasted flavor and softer texture, try baking it with the tortilla strips. Place the strips at one end of the baking pan and the corn at the other end.

mexican FIESTA SALAD

Start to Finish: 30 minutes
Makes: 4 servings

2 cups dried penne or rotini pasta

½ cup frozen whole kernel corn

½ cup light sour cream

⅓ cup mild or medium chunky salsa

1 tablespoon snipped fresh cilantro

1 tablespoon lime juice

1 15-ounce can black beans, rinsed and drained

3 medium roma tomatoes, chopped (1 cup)

1 medium zucchini, chopped (1 cup)

½ cup shredded sharp cheddar cheese (2 ounces)

1 Cook pasta according to package directions, adding corn for the last 5 minutes of cooking; drain. Rinse with cold water; drain again.

2 Meanwhile, for dressing, in a small bowl stir together sour cream, salsa, cilantro, and lime juice.

3 In a large bowl, combine the pasta mixture, black beans, tomatoes, zucchini, and cheddar cheese. Pour the dressing over pasta mixture; toss gently to coat.

4 Serve immediately or cover and refrigerate up to 24 hours. (After chilling, if necessary, stir in enough milk to thin dressing to desired consistency.)

Nutrition facts per serving: 373 cal., 9 g total fat (4 g sat. fat), 19 mg chol., 470 mg sodium, 61 g carb., 7 g dietary fiber, 20 g protein.

asian TOFU SALAD

Prep: 20 minutes
Marinate: 30 minutes
Cook: 5 minutes
Makes: 6 servings
(1¼ cups salad
with 2 slices tofu
per serving)

¼ cup reduced-sodium soy sauce

¼ cup sweet chili sauce

1 tablespoon creamy peanut butter

1 clove garlic, minced

1 teaspoon grated fresh ginger

1 16- to 18-ounce package firm water-packed tofu

1 teaspoon toasted sesame oil

4 cups shredded romaine lettuce

1½ cups chopped peeled jicama

1 medium red sweet pepper, seeded and thinly sliced

1 cup coarsely shredded carrots

2 tablespoons unsalted dry-roasted peanuts

2 tablespoons snipped fresh cilantro

1 In a small bowl, whisk together soy sauce, chili sauce, peanut butter, garlic, and ginger. Pat tofu dry with paper towels. Cut tofu crosswise into 12 slices. Place slices in a 2-quart rectangular baking dish. Drizzle tofu with 3 tablespoons of the soy sauce mixture, turning to coat tofu. Let marinate for 30 minutes, turning tofu occasionally. Set aside the remaining soy sauce mixture for dressing.

2 In a very large nonstick skillet, heat sesame oil over medium-high heat. Remove tofu slices from the marinade. Add remaining marinade to the skillet. Add tofu slices to the hot skillet. Cook for 5 to 6 minutes or until lightly browned, turning once halfway through cooking.

3 In a large bowl, combine lettuce, jicama, sweet pepper, and carrot. Divide among serving plates. Top with tofu, peanuts, and cilantro. Serve with reserved dressing mixture.

Nutrition facts per serving: 179 cal., 7 g total fat (1 g sat. fat), 0 mg chol., 515 mg sodium, 18 g carb., 3 g dietary fiber, 11 g protein.

thai BULGUR SALAD

Prep: 25 minutes
Cook: 15 minutes
Makes: 4 servings

1   cup water
½   cup bulgur
2   cups fresh or frozen
    sweet soybeans
    (edamame), thawed
1   medium red sweet
    pepper, seeded and cut
    into thin bite-size strips
½   cup coarsely shredded
    carrot
½   cup thinly sliced red
    onion
2   tablespoons snipped
    fresh cilantro
4   cups fresh spinach leaves
    Thai Peanut Dressing*
¼   cup chopped peanuts
    (optional)

1 In a medium saucepan, bring the water to boiling; add bulgur. Return to boiling; reduce heat. Cover and simmer for about 15 minutes or until bulgur is tender and most of the liquid is absorbed. Drain, if necessary. Transfer to a large bowl; stir in soybeans, sweet pepper, carrot, red onion, and cilantro.

2 Divide spinach among serving plates. Top with bulgur mixture; drizzle with Thai Peanut Dressing. If desired, sprinkle with peanuts.

*Thai Peanut Dressing: In a small saucepan, combine ⅓ cup water, ¼ cup creamy peanut butter, 2 tablespoons reduced-sodium soy sauce, 1 teaspoon sugar, ¼ teaspoon ground ginger, ⅛ teaspoon crushed red pepper, and 1 clove garlic, minced. Whisk constantly over medium-low heat for about 3 minutes or until smooth and slightly thickened (mixture will appear curdled at first, but will become smooth as it is whisked over the heat). Makes ⅔ cup.

Nutrition facts per serving: 381 cal., 17 g total fat (3 g sat. fat), 0 mg chol., 420 mg sodium, 38 g carb., 12 g dietary fiber, 25 g protein.

tabbouleh WITH EDAMAME AND FETA

Start to Finish: 25 minutes
Makes: 6 servings

2½ **cups water**

1¼ **cups bulgur**

¼ **cup lemon juice**

3 **tablespoons purchased basil pesto**

2 **cups fresh or thawed frozen sweet soybeans (edamame)**

2 **cups cherry tomatoes, cut up**

⅓ **cup crumbled reduced-fat feta cheese**

⅓ **cup thinly sliced scallions**

2 **tablespoons snipped fresh parsley**

¼ **teaspoon ground black pepper**

Fresh parsley sprigs (optional)

1 In a medium saucepan, bring the water to boiling; add bulgur. Return to boiling; reduce heat. Cover and simmer for about 15 minutes or until most of the liquid is absorbed. Remove from heat. Transfer to a large bowl.

2 In a small bowl, whisk together lemon juice and pesto. Add to bulgur along with soybeans, cherry tomatoes, feta cheese, scallions, the snipped parsley, and pepper. Toss gently to combine. If desired, garnish with parsley sprigs.

Nutrition facts per serving: 266 cal., 10 g total fat (1 g sat. fat), 3 mg chol., 181 mg sodium, 34 g carb., 9 g dietary fiber, 14 g protein.

Make-Ahead Directions: Prepare as directed. Cover and chill for up to 4 hours.

wheat BERRY SALAD

Prep: 20 minutes
Cook: 40 minutes
Cool: 1 hour
Makes: 4 servings

2½ **cups water**

1 **cup wheat berries, rinsed**

2 **tablespoons lemon juice**

2 **tablespoons canola oil**

1 **tablespoon maple syrup**

¼ **teaspoon ground cinnamon**

¼ **teaspoon salt**

¼ **teaspoon ground black pepper**

1 **medium apple, cored, peeled, and sliced**

1 **large carrot, shredded**

2 **scallions, sliced**

6 **cups fresh baby spinach**

¼ **cup snipped dried apricots**

1 In a small saucepan, bring the water to boiling. Add wheat berries to boiling water. Return to boiling; reduce heat. Cover and simmer for 40 to 50 minutes or until tender. Drain and transfer to a large bowl. Let cool for 1 hour.

2 In a small bowl, whisk together lemon juice, oil, syrup, cinnamon, salt, and pepper. Drizzle dressing over cooled wheat berries. Add apple, carrot, and scallions; toss to coat. Serve wheat berry mixture over baby spinach; sprinkle with dried apricots.

Nutrition facts per serving: 284 cal., 8 g total fat (1 g sat. fat), 0 mg chol., 217 mg sodium, 50 g carb., 12 g dietary fiber, 8 g protein.

tarragon BEAN SALAD

Start to Finish: 20 minutes
Makes: 5 servings

1 15-ounce can red kidney beans, rinsed and drained

1 15-ounce can butter beans, rinsed and drained

1 15-ounce can garbanzo beans, rinsed and drained

1½ cups chopped seeded tomatoes or halved cherry or grape tomatoes

1 medium carrot, cut into thin bite-size strips

2 tablespoons finely chopped red onion

3 tablespoons olive oil

2 tablespoons red wine vinegar

2 tablespoons Dijon-style mustard

1 tablespoon snipped fresh tarragon, or ½ teaspoon dried tarragon, crushed

1 teaspoon sugar

¼ teaspoon salt

⅛ teaspoon ground black pepper

Boston lettuce leaves

1 In a large bowl, combine beans, tomatoes, carrot, and red onion. For dressing, in a screw-top jar combine oil, vinegar, mustard, tarragon, sugar, salt, and black pepper. Cover and shake well.

2 Pour the dressing over bean mixture; toss gently to coat. Serve the salad on lettuce-lined dinner plates.

Nutrition facts per serving: 334 cal., 10 g total fat (1 g sat. fat), 0 mg chol., 1005 mg sodium, 49 g carb., 13 g dietary fiber, 14 g protein.

greek GARBANZO SALAD

Prep: 25 minutes
Chill: 4 to 24 hours
Makes: 4 servings

1   15-ounce can garbanzo
    beans (chickpeas), rinsed
    and drained

2   medium tomatoes, cut
    into chunks

1   large cucumber, seeded
    and chopped (about
    2 cups)

1   cup coarsely chopped
    green sweet pepper

½   cup thinly sliced red
    onion

2   tablespoons olive oil

2   tablespoons red wine
    vinegar

1   tablespoon snipped
    fresh mint

1   tablespoon lemon juice

2   cloves garlic, minced

½   cup crumbled reduced-fat
    feta cheese (2 ounces)

    Salt and ground black
    pepper

2   cups packaged mixed
    salad greens

1 In a large bowl, combine garbanzo beans, tomatoes, cucumber, sweet pepper, and red onion.

2 In a small bowl, whisk together oil, red wine vinegar, mint, lemon juice, and garlic. Pour over garbanzo bean mixture; toss to coat. Cover and chill for 4 to 24 hours.

3 Stir in feta cheese. Season to taste with salt and black pepper. Serve over mixed greens.

Nutrition facts per serving: 200 cal., 10 g total fat (3 g sat. fat), 5 mg chol., 694 mg sodium, 25 g carb., 7 g dietary fiber, 11 g protein.

black bean SLAW WITH SOY-GINGER DRESSING

Start to Finish: 20 minutes
Makes: 4 servings

- **1 15-ounce can black beans, rinsed and drained**
- **6 cups packaged shredded cabbage with carrot (coleslaw mix)**
- **2 medium green apples, cored and chopped**
- **1 large red sweet pepper, cut into strips**
- **¼ cup cider vinegar**
- **2 tablespoons reduced-sodium soy sauce**
- **2 tablespoons peanut oil**
- **2 teaspoons grated fresh ginger**
- **2 teaspoons honey**
- **¼ teaspoon ground black pepper**

In a large bowl, combine black beans, shredded cabbage with carrot, apples, and sweet pepper. In a small screw-top jar, combine cider vinegar, soy sauce, peanut oil, ginger, honey, and black pepper; cover and shake well. Pour over cabbage mixture. Toss to coat.

Nutrition facts per serving: 217 cal., 7 g total fat (1 g sat. fat), 0 mg chol., 577 mg sodium, 36 g carb., 9 g dietary fiber, 9 g protein.

salsa, BLACK BEAN, AND RICE SALAD

Start to Finish: 25 minutes
Makes: 6 servings

2 cups chopped romaine lettuce

2 cups cooked brown rice, chilled

1 15-ounce can black beans, rinsed and drained

2 cups chopped tomatoes

1 cup chopped green, yellow, and/or red sweet pepper

1 cup loose-pack frozen whole kernel corn, thawed

2 scallions, thinly sliced

2 tablespoons snipped fresh cilantro

1 cup purchased picante sauce or salsa

4 ounces Monterey Jack cheese with jalapeño chile peppers, cut into ¼-inch cubes (optional)

½ cup light sour cream

In a large bowl, stir together lettuce, rice, black beans, tomatoes, sweet pepper, corn, scallions, and cilantro; add picante sauce or salsa. Toss to coat. If desired, stir in cheese. Serve with sour cream.

Nutrition facts per serving: 201 cal., 3 g total fat (1 g sat. fat), 6 mg chol., 469 mg sodium, 39 g carb., 7 g dietary fiber, 9 g protein.

blue cheese AND BEAN SALAD

Prep: 15 minutes
Chill: 4 to 24 hours
Bake: 5 minutes
Oven: 350°F
Makes: 6 servings

2 **15-ounce cans navy beans, rinsed and drained**

1 **small zucchini, quartered lengthwise and cut into ¼-inch slices (1 cup)**

2 **small tomatoes, seeded and coarsely chopped**

2 **scallions, thinly sliced**

⅓ **cup white wine vinegar**

2 **tablespoons olive oil**

¼ **teaspoon dried Italian seasoning, crushed**

⅛ **teaspoon ground black pepper**

2 **cups French bread cut into ¾-inch cubes**

   Butter-flavored nonstick cooking spray

½ **teaspoon onion powder**

½ **teaspoon garlic powder**

¼ **cup crumbled blue cheese (1 ounce)**

① In a large bowl, combine navy beans, zucchini, tomatoes, and scallions.

② For dressing, in a screw-top jar combine vinegar, olive oil, Italian seasoning, and pepper. Cover and shake well. Pour dressing over bean mixture, tossing to coat. Cover and chill for 4 to 24 hours, stirring once or twice.

③ For croutons, before serving salad, preheat oven to 350°F. Arrange bread cubes in a single layer in a 15x10x1-inch baking pan. Spray bread cubes with cooking spray; toss to coat. Sprinkle with onion powder and garlic powder; toss to coat. Bake for 5 to 7 minutes or until golden brown, stirring twice. Add croutons and blue cheese to the bean mixture; toss gently. Serve immediately.

Nutrition facts per serving: 265 cal., 7 g total fat (2 g sat. fat), 4 mg chol., 782 mg sodium, 40 g carb., 1 g dietary fiber, 13 g protein.

sandwiches

open-face RATATOUILLE SANDWICH

Eggplant, zucchini, and squash are all high in nutrients and fill you up, but they are low in calories, making them ideal for lunch.

Prep: 25 minutes
Roast: 45 minutes
Oven: 400°F
Makes: 4 servings

1 **small eggplant, cut into 1-inch pieces**

1 **small zucchini or yellow summer squash, cut into ¾-inch slices**

1 **medium red sweet pepper, cut into strips**

½ **of a small red onion, cut into ½-inch wedges**

1 **tablespoon olive oil**

½ **teaspoon herbes de Provence or dried thyme, crushed**

⅛ **teaspoon salt**

⅛ **teaspoon ground black pepper**

2 **medium roma tomatoes, each cut lengthwise into 6 wedges**

8 **small or 4 large ½-inch slices whole wheat or white French bread, toasted (about 8 ounces total)**

1 **clove garlic, halved**

2 **tablespoons balsamic vinegar**

Fresh thyme sprigs (optional)

1 Preheat oven to 400°F. Coat a large shallow roasting pan with nonstick cooking spray. Add eggplant, zucchini, sweet pepper, and onion to prepared pan. Drizzle with olive oil; sprinkle with herbes de Provence, salt, and black pepper. Toss to coat. Roast vegetables for 30 minutes, tossing once. Add tomatoes to roasting pan. Roast for 15 to 20 minutes more or until vegetables are tender and some surface areas are lightly browned.

2 Meanwhile, rub toasted bread with cut sides of the garlic clove. Place 2 small slices or 1 large slice of the bread on each serving plate. Sprinkle balsamic vinegar over vegetables; toss gently to coat. Spoon warm vegetables on bread. If desired, garnish with fresh thyme sprigs.

Nutrition facts per serving: 250 cal., 7 g total fat (1 g sat. fat), 0 mg chol., 328 mg sodium, 43 g carb., 8 g dietary fiber, 7 g protein.

sautéed ONION AND TOMATO SANDWICHES

Start to Finish: 20 minutes
Makes: 4 servings

2 **medium onions, sliced**

1 **teaspoon olive oil**

8 **slices hearty whole grain
   or rye bread (toasted,
   if desired)**

Honey mustard

3 **small red and/or yellow
   tomatoes, thinly sliced**

4 **lettuce leaves, shredded**

Small fresh basil leaves

4 **ounces spreadable Brie
   cheese or tub-style
   cream cheese**

1 In a large skillet, cook onions in hot oil over medium-high heat for 5 to 7 minutes or until onions are tender and just starting to brown, stirring frequently. Remove from heat; cool slightly.

2 To assemble, lightly spread one side of 4 bread slices with honey mustard. Top with onion slices, tomato slices, shredded lettuce, and basil. Spread one side of the remaining 4 bread slices with Brie cheese. Place the bread slices, cheese side down, on top of sandwiches.

Nutrition facts per serving: 287 cal., 12 g total fat (6 g sat. fat), 28 mg chol., 490 mg sodium, 35 g carb., 1 g dietary fiber, 12 g protein.

pepper STROMZONI

Prep: 30 minutes
Bake: 15 minutes
Stand: 10 minutes
Oven: 400°F
Makes: 4 servings

- 3 **medium red, yellow, and/or green sweet peppers, chopped (3 cups)**
- 6 **cloves garlic, minced**
- 1 **tablespoon butter**
- ½ **teaspoon salt**
- ¼ **teaspoon ground black pepper**
- ¼ **to ½ teaspoon crushed red pepper**
- ¾ **cup shredded mozzarella cheese (3 ounces)**
- ½ **cup ricotta cheese**
- 2 **tablespoon snipped fresh basil**
- 1 **13.8-ounce package refrigerated pizza dough**
- 1 **egg, lightly beaten**

1. Preheat oven to 400°F. Line a large baking sheet with foil or parchment paper; grease foil and set aside. In a large skillet, cook sweet peppers and garlic in hot butter over medium heat for about 5 minutes or until tender, stirring occasionally. Stir in the salt, black pepper, and crushed red pepper; let cool.

2. In a medium bowl, stir together mozzarella, ricotta, and basil. Stir pepper mixture into cheese mixture until well combined. On a lightly floured surface, roll out pizza dough to a 16x10-inch rectangle. Cut into two 10x8-inch rectangles. Spoon half of the pepper mixture along one of the long sides of one dough rectangle, leaving a 1-inch border along the long side and a ½-inch border along the short sides. Spread pepper mixture to a width of about 3 inches. Fold one long side over the pepper mixture. Seal seam and ends, tucking seam under the loaf. Carefully place on prepared baking sheet. Repeat with remaining dough and filling.

3. With a sharp knife, cut 4 diagonal slits in the top of each loaf. Brush loaves with egg. Bake for 15 to 18 minutes or until golden brown. Let stand for 10 minutes. Slice each in half and serve warm.

Nutrition facts per serving: 365 cal., 14 g total fat (7 g sat. fat), 89 mg chol., 855 mg sodium, 42 g carb., 3 g dietary fiber, 17 g protein.

artichoke AND BASIL HERO

Start to Finish: 30 minutes
Makes: 6 servings

1 **cup fresh basil leaves**

¼ **cup olive oil or salad oil**

2 **tablespoons grated Parmesan cheese**

1 **tablespoon capers, drained**

1 **tablespoon white wine vinegar**

2 **teaspoons Dijon-style mustard**

1 **clove garlic, quartered**

1 **16-ounce loaf unsliced French bread**

1 **14-ounce can artichoke hearts, drained and sliced**

4 **ounces sliced provolone cheese**

1 **medium tomato, thinly sliced**

2 **cups torn fresh spinach**

1 In a blender container or food processor bowl, combine basil, oil, Parmesan cheese, capers, vinegar, mustard, and garlic. Cover; blend or process until nearly smooth.

2 Cut bread in half lengthwise. Hollow out each half, leaving a ½- to 1-inch shell. (Save bread crumbs for another use.) Spread the basil mixture over cut side of each bread half. On the bottom half, layer artichoke hearts, provolone cheese, tomato, and spinach. Cover with top half of bread. Cut sandwich crosswise into 6 pieces.

Nutrition facts per serving: 396 cal., 17 g total fat (5 g sat. fat), 14 mg chol., 887 mg sodium, 46 g carb., 4 g dietary fiber, 15 g protein.

peppery ARTICHOKE PITAS

Black-eyed peas add texture and substance to these vegetarian pita pockets.

Start to Finish: 20 minutes
Makes: 6 sandwiches

1 **15-ounce can black-eyed peas, rinsed and drained**

1 **13.75- to 14-ounce can artichoke hearts, drained and cut up**

½ **cup packaged torn mixed salad greens**

¼ **cup bottled creamy Italian salad dressing or creamy garlic salad dressing**

¼ **teaspoon ground black pepper**

1 **small tomato, sliced**

3 **pita bread rounds, halved crosswise***

In a medium bowl, combine black-eyed peas, artichoke hearts, mixed greens, salad dressing, and pepper. Place tomato slices inside pita bread halves. Spoon artichoke mixture into pita bread halves.

Nutrition facts per sandwich: 211 cal., 5 g total fat (1 g sat. fat), 0 mg chol., 746 mg sodium, 34 g carb., 6 g dietary fiber, 8 g protein.

*Tip: For softer pita breads, wrap the pita bread rounds in foil and warm in a 350°F oven for 10 minutes. Soft pita bread rounds are easier to split.

tofu PITAS WITH MANGO SALSA

Although the ingredients for Jamaican jerk seasoning differ from brand to brand, this Caribbean flavoring blend typically includes chile peppers, thyme, spices, and garlic. Look for it in the seasoning aisle of your supermarket.

Prep: 35 minutes
Marinate: 30 minutes
Grill: 10 minutes
Makes: 6 servings

- 2 tablespoons lime juice or lemon juice
- 1 teaspoon cooking oil
- ½ teaspoon purchased Jamaican jerk seasoning
- 1 10.5-ounce package firm light tofu
- Nonstick cooking spray
- ⅓ cup couscous
- Mango Salsa*
- 3 large pita bread rounds, halved crosswise
- Spinach leaves or torn lettuce leaves
- Lime slices (optional)

1 For marinade, in a shallow dish combine the lime juice, oil, and Jamaican jerk seasoning. Cut tofu into ½-inch slices. Place tofu slices in marinade and brush marinade over slices. Marinate at room temperature for 30 minutes, turning slices once and brushing with marinade, or marinate in the refrigerator for up to 6 hours.

2 Coat a grill basket with cooking spray. Place tofu slices in prepared grill basket. Discard marinade. Place basket with tofu slices on the rack of an uncovered grill directly over medium-hot coals. Grill for about 10 minutes or until heated through, turning once. (Or, coat the unheated rack of a broiler pan with cooking spray. Place tofu on prepared rack. Broil 5 to 6 inches from the heat for about 8 minutes or until heated through, turning once.) Cut the tofu slices into cubes.

3 Meanwhile, cook couscous according to package directions, except omit any butter or salt. Fluff with a fork.

4 To serve, add tofu cubes and couscous to Mango Salsa; toss gently to mix. Line pita halves with spinach. Spoon tofu mixture into pita halves. If desired, serve with lime slices.

*Mango Salsa: In a medium bowl combine 1 cup peeled and chopped mango; 1 small tomato, seeded and chopped; ½ of a medium cucumber, seeded and chopped; 1 thinly sliced scallion; 2 tablespoons snipped fresh cilantro; 1 fresh jalapeño pepper, seeded and chopped; and 1 tablespoon lime or lemon juice. Cover and chill until serving time. Makes about 2 cups.

Nutrition facts per serving: 175 cal., 2 g total fat (0 g sat. fat), 0 mg chol., 214 mg sodium, 33 g carb., 3 g dietary fiber, 7 g protein.

spinach PANINI

Prep: 20 minutes
Cook: 2 minutes per batch
Makes: 4 servings

4 **6-inch whole wheat hoagie rolls, split; 8 slices whole wheat bread; or 2 whole wheat pita bread rounds, halved crosswise and split horizontally**

4 **cups fresh baby spinach leaves**

8 **thin tomato slices (1 medium)**

¼ **teaspoon kosher salt**

⅛ **teaspoon ground black pepper**

¼ **cup thinly sliced red onion**

2 **tablespoons shredded fresh basil leaves**

½ **cup crumbled feta cheese (2 ounces)**

1 Lightly coat an unheated panini griddle, covered indoor electric grill, or large nonstick skillet with cooking spray. Preheat over medium heat or heat according to manufacturer's directions.

2 Place hoagie roll bottoms on a work surface; divide 2 cups of the spinach leaves among roll bottoms. Top with tomato and sprinkle lightly with kosher salt and pepper. Add red onion slices and basil. Top with feta, the remaining 2 cups spinach, and hoagie roll tops. Press down firmly.

3 Add sandwiches, in batches if necessary. If using griddle or grill, close lid and grill for 2 to 3 minutes or until bread is toasted. If using skillet, place a heavy plate on top of sandwiches. Cook for 1 to 2 minutes or until bottoms are toasted. Carefully remove plate, which may be hot. Turn sandwiches and top with the plate. Cook for 1 to 2 minutes more or until bread is toasted. Serve immediately.

Nutrition facts per serving: 299 cal., 7 g total fat (3 g sat. fat), 13 mg chol., 826 mg sodium, 50 g carb., 8 g dietary fiber, 13 g protein.

eggplant PANINI

Why say sandwich *when you can say* panini? *The Italian word sounds so much more enticing, with a promise of unexpected delights—even if it does simply mean "bread roll" in Italian!*

Start to Finish: 25 minutes
Makes: 6 servings

- 1 **cup torn arugula**
- 2 **teaspoons red wine vinegar**
- 1 **teaspoon olive oil**
- ⅓ **cup seasoned fine dry bread crumbs**
- 2 **tablespoons grated Pecorino Romano or Parmesan cheese**
- 1 **egg**
- 1 **tablespoon milk**
- 2 **tablespoons all-purpose flour**
- ½ **teaspoon salt**
- 1 **medium eggplant, cut crosswise into ½-inch slices**
- 1 **tablespoon olive oil**
- 3 **ounces fresh mozzarella cheese, thinly sliced**
- 1 **12-inch plain or seasoned Italian flatbread (focaccia),* halved horizontally**
- 1 **large tomato, thinly sliced**

1 In a small bowl, toss together the arugula, vinegar, and the 1 teaspoon oil; set aside. In a shallow dish, stir together the bread crumbs and Romano cheese. In another shallow dish, beat together the egg and milk. In a third shallow dish, stir together the flour and salt. Dip the eggplant slices into flour mixture to coat. Dip the slices into egg mixture, then coat both sides with crumb mixture.

2 In a 12-inch nonstick skillet, heat the 1 tablespoon oil over medium heat. Add eggplant slices; cook for 6 to 8 minutes or until lightly browned, turning once. (Add more oil as necessary during cooking.) Top the eggplant with mozzarella cheese; reduce heat to low. Cook, covered, just until cheese begins to melt.

3 To serve, place the eggplant slices, cheese side up, on bottom half of bread. Top with the arugula mixture, tomato slices, and top half of bread. Cut into wedges.

Nutrition facts per serving: 318 cal., 10 g total fat (4 g sat. fat), 48 mg chol., 447 mg sodium, 45 g carb., 5 g dietary fiber, 13 g protein.

*Tip: For easier slicing, purchase focaccia that is at least 2½ inches thick.

spinach-mushroom
QUESADILLAS

Prep: 25 minutes
Cook: 2 minutes per batch
Oven: 300°F
Makes: 4 servings

- **1 tablespoon olive oil**
- **½ of a medium red onion, thinly sliced (½ cup)**
- **2 cloves garlic, minced**
- **8 ounces fresh portobello mushrooms, coarsely chopped**
- **1 9-ounce package fresh spinach (8 to 10 cups)**
- **½ cup grated reduced-fat Parmesan cheese**
- **½ cup shredded part-skim mozzarella cheese (2 ounces)**
- **2 tablespoons snipped fresh basil, or 2 teaspoons dried basil, crushed**
- **4 7- or 8-inch whole wheat flour tortillas**
- **Olive oil nonstick cooking spray**

1 Preheat oven to 300°F. In a large skillet, heat oil over medium heat. Add onion and garlic; cook for 5 minutes, stirring occasionally. Add mushrooms; cook for about 5 minutes more or until almost tender, stirring occasionally. Add spinach in batches; cook and stir just until spinach is wilted before adding more. When all spinach is just wilted, remove from heat. Stir in Parmesan cheese, mozzarella cheese, and basil. Remove spinach mixture from skillet. Set skillet aside to cool.

2 Divide spinach mixture among tortillas, spooning it on half of each tortilla. Fold each tortilla over spinach mixture, pressing gently. Lightly coat both sides of each quesadilla with nonstick cooking spray. Rinse out and dry the skillet.

3 Heat skillet over medium heat. Place 2 of the quesadillas in the hot skillet; cook for 2 to 3 minutes or until lightly browned, turning once. Remove quesadillas from skillet; place on baking sheet. Keep warm in oven. Repeat with remaining 2 quesadillas. Cut quesadillas in half to serve.

Nutrition facts per serving: 293 cal., 12 g total fat (4 g sat. fat), 21 mg chol., 701 mg sodium, 29 g carb., 13 g dietary fiber, 18 g protein.

grilled VEGETABLES ON FOCACCIA

A blend of goat cheese and cream cheese is spread over focaccia and filled with a colorful mix of grilled red sweet peppers, zucchini, and eggplant in this vegetarian sandwich.

Prep: 25 minutes
Grill: 8 minutes
Makes: 8 servings

3 tablespoons balsamic vinegar or wine vinegar

2 tablespoons water

1 tablespoon olive oil

1 teaspoon dried oregano, crushed

2 large red and/or yellow sweet peppers

2 medium zucchini, halved crosswise and sliced thinly lengthwise

1 medium eggplant, cut crosswise into ½-inch slices

1 12-inch round purchased focaccia

2 ounces soft goat cheese

2 ounces fat-free cream cheese

1 For the vinaigrette,* combine balsamic vinegar, water, olive oil, and oregano in a small bowl.

2 Cut sweet peppers in quarters. Remove stems, membranes, and seeds. Arrange all vegetables on grill rack directly over medium-hot coals; brush with vinaigrette. Grill, uncovered, until slightly charred, turning occasionally (allow 8 to 10 minutes for peppers and eggplant, 5 to 6 minutes for zucchini). Cut peppers into strips.

3 Cut focaccia in half crosswise. Split halves into 2 layers horizontally to form 4 pieces total. Combine goat cheese and cream cheese, and spread over bottom layers of focaccia; top with the sweet pepper, zucchini, and eggplant; place top halves of focaccia over vegetables. To serve, cut each focaccia half into 4 wedges.

Nutrition facts per serving: 201 cal., 5 g total fat (2 g sat. fat), 4 mg chol., 68 mg sodium, 32 g carb., 4 g dietary fiber, 8 g protein.

*Tip: If you like, use ⅓ cup purchased, bottled Italian dressing instead of preparing the vinaigrette.

garden VEGGIE BURGERS

Two toppings—sharp red onion and a tangy spinach-feta combination—complement these grilled meatless burgers.

Prep: 10 minutes
Grill: 15 minutes
Makes: 4 servings

- 2 **medium red onions**
- 4 **refrigerated or frozen meatless burger patties**
- ¼ **cup bottled vinaigrette salad dressing (room temperature)**
- 4 **cups spinach leaves**
- 1 **clove garlic, minced**
- 1 **tablespoon olive oil**
- ½ **cup crumbled feta cheese (2 ounces)**
- 4 **hamburger buns**

1 For onion topping, cut onions into ½-inch slices. Place onions on the rack of an uncovered grill directly over medium coals. Grill for 15 to 20 minutes or until tender, turning once. Add the meatless patties to grill alongside onions; grill for 8 to 10 minutes or until heated through, turning once. Brush the grilled onions with the salad dressing.

2 For spinach topping, in a large skillet cook and stir the spinach and garlic in hot olive oil over medium-high heat for about 30 seconds or just until spinach is wilted. Remove from heat. Stir in the feta cheese.

3 To serve, place onion slices on bottoms of buns. Top with the grilled burgers, spinach topping, and bun tops.

Nutrition facts per serving: 350 cal., 14 g total fat (4 g sat. fat), 17 mg chol., 920 mg sodium, 37 g carb., 7 g dietary fiber, 21 g protein.

zucchini-carrot BURGERS

Who needs fast food with these appetizing veggie burgers, a nutrient- and fiber-filled alternative to meat? Serve them in whole wheat pita bread for even more whole grain goodness.

Start to Finish: 25 minutes
Makes: 4 servings

- 1 **lightly beaten egg, or ¼ cup refrigerated or frozen egg product, thawed**
- 1 **tablespoon olive oil**
- 1 **teaspoon dried oregano, crushed**
- 1 **cup crushed stone-ground wheat crackers (about 22)**
- 1 **cup finely shredded zucchini**
- 1 **cup finely shredded carrots**
- ¼ **cup chopped scallions**
- ½ **cup low-fat plain yogurt**
- 2 **cloves garlic, minced**
- ½ **teaspoon finely shredded lemon zest**
- 2 **large whole wheat pita bread rounds, halved crosswise**
- 1 **cup shredded leaf lettuce**
- 1 **small tomato, thinly sliced**
- ½ **of a small cucumber, thinly sliced**

1 In a medium bowl, combine egg, 1 teaspoon of the oil, and the oregano. Add crushed crackers, zucchini, carrots, and scallions; mix well. Form the vegetable mixture into 4 patties, each about 3½ inches in diameter.

2 In a large nonstick skillet, heat the remaining 2 teaspoons oil over medium heat. Add patties to skillet. Cook for 5 to 7 minutes or until patties are golden brown, turning once halfway through cooking time.

3 Meanwhile, for sauce, in a small bowl combine yogurt, garlic, and lemon zest.

4 To serve, place each vegetable patty in a pita bread half. Add lettuce, tomato, cucumber, and sauce.

Nutrition facts per serving: 284 cal., 10 g total fat (2 g sat. fat), 55 mg chol., 378 mg sodium, 41 g carb., 6 g dietary fiber, 10 g protein.

bean BURGERS

Prep: 10 minutes
Grill: 10 minutes
Makes: 6 servings

2   15.5-ounce cans pinto
    beans, drained
    and rinsed*
½   cup dry fine bread crumbs
½   cup bottled salsa
1   egg
1   teaspoon chili powder
½   teaspoon ground cumin
½   cup coarsely crushed
    baked tortilla chips
    Nonstick cooking spray
3   4-inch pitas, halved
12 lettuce leaves
12 slices tomato
    Bottled salsa

1 Prepare charcoal grill with medium-hot coals or heat gas grill to medium-high (or heat oven broiler). Lightly coat grill rack or broiler pan rack with nonstick cooking spray.

2 Reserve 1 cup of the pinto beans. Whirl remaining beans in a food processor or mash with fork in large bowl until smooth.

3 In large bowl, combine the reserved 1 cup beans, the pureed beans, bread crumbs, the ½ cup salsa, egg, chili powder and cumin. Stir in crushed chips. Shape into 6 patties. Coat both sides of each patty with nonstick cooking spray.

4 Grill or broil about 4 inches from heat, turning once, for about 10 minutes or until instant-read thermometer inserted in centers registers 160°F. Serve in pita pocket halves with lettuce and tomato slices. Serve with additional salsa.

Nutrition facts per serving: 234 cal., 3 g total fat (1 g sat. fat), 36 mg chol., 994 mg sodium, 41 g carb., 5 g dietary fiber, 10 g protein.

*Tip: Ready to use in recipes, canned beans save you time. However, with their added salt, they can tip the scale on sodium in recipes. Rinsing and draining beans in a colander under cold running water helps eliminate the salty packing liquid. Be sure to drain the beans well.

italian VEGGIE BURGER BITES

Start to Finish: 15 minutes
Makes: 4 servings

4 refrigerated or frozen
   meatless burger patties

¼ cup tomato paste

4 to 5 tablespoons water

2 teaspoons snipped
   fresh basil

8 slices firm-textured whole
   wheat or oatmeal bread,
   toasted, if desired

4 slices mozzarella cheese
   (1 ounce)

16 small fresh basil leaves

1 Cook burger patties according to package directions. Meanwhile, for sauce, in a small bowl combine tomato paste, water, and snipped basil.

2 To serve, place each burger patty on 1 slice of bread. Top with sauce, cheese, and basil leaves. Top with another slice of bread. If desired, cut each sandwich into quarters.

Nutrition facts per serving: 332 cal., 12 g total fat (2 g sat. fat), 25 mg chol., 819 mg sodium, 33 g carb., 8 g dietary fiber, 26 g protein.

Tomato-Mayo Veggie Burger Bites: Prepare as above except omit tomato paste, water, basil, and cheese. In a small bowl, combine ¼ cup mayonnaise or salad dressing, 3 tablespoons ketchup, and pinch of garlic powder. Top each burger with some of the ketchup mixture and a lettuce leaf. Serve as above.

Barbecue Veggie Burger Bites: Prepare as above except omit tomato paste, water, basil, and cheese. Top each burger with 1 rounded tablespoon bottled barbecue sauce and a lettuce leaf. Serve as above.

ginger TOFU SALAD WRAPS

Tofu absorbs the great variety of nutty, spicy, and sour ingredients of the marinade and brings added texture to this unconventional sandwich.

Prep: 30 minutes
Marinate: 30 minutes
Makes: 4 servings

1 12- to 14-ounce package firm or extra-firm tofu

4 scallions, sliced

2 tablespoons reduced-sodium soy sauce

1 tablespoon rice vinegar

1 teaspoon toasted sesame oil

1 teaspoon grated fresh ginger

2 cloves garlic, minced

⅛ teaspoon ground red pepper

¼ cup finely chopped red sweet pepper

8 8-inch round rice papers

Arugula leaves

Soy sauce (optional)

1 If necessary, drain tofu. Cut into ½-inch cubes. Place the tofu and scallions in a medium bowl.

2 For marinade, in a screw-top jar combine the soy sauce, rice vinegar, sesame oil, ginger, garlic, and ground red pepper. Cover and shake well. Pour over tofu mixture; toss gently to coat. Cover and marinate at room temperature for 30 minutes. Gently stir in red sweet pepper; set aside.

3 Meanwhile, quickly dip each rice paper in water and place between damp cotton kitchen towels. Let stand for about 10 minutes to soften.

4 To assemble, remove a rice paper from between towels. Place some arugula leaves and about ⅓ cup of the tofu mixture on rice paper just below center. Roll up just enough to enclose filling. Fold 2 sides of rice paper over filling; continue rolling up. Repeat with the remaining rice papers, arugula, and tofu mixture. If desired, serve with additional soy sauce.

Nutrition facts per serving: 163 cal., 4 g total fat (1 g sat. fat), 0 mg chol., 306 mg sodium, 24 g carb., 2 g dietary fiber, 8 g protein.

Make-Ahead Directions: Assemble the wraps, cover, and refrigerate for up to 1 hour before serving.

white bean AND
GOAT CHEESE WRAPS

These no-cook bean-and-cheese wraps are perfect picnic food. Roll them tightly in plastic wrap or foil and keep them cool until it's time to eat.

Start to Finish: 20 minutes
Makes: 6 servings

1   19-ounce can cannellini beans (white kidney beans), rinsed and drained

1   4-ounce package soft goat cheese

1   tablespoon chopped fresh oregano

1   tablespoon chopped fresh parsley

6   8-inch whole wheat flour tortillas, warmed, if desired*

6   cups fresh baby spinach leaves

1   12-ounce jar roasted red sweet peppers, drained and thinly sliced

1 In a medium bowl, mash beans lightly with a fork. Add goat cheese, oregano, and parsley; stir until well mixed.

2 Divide bean mixture among tortillas, spreading evenly. Top bean mixture with spinach and roasted peppers. Roll up tortillas; cut in half to serve.

Nutrition facts per serving: 248 cal., 8 g total fat (4 g sat. fat), 9 mg chol., 552 mg sodium, 31 g carb., 16 g dietary fiber, 18 g protein.

*Tip: To warm tortillas, preheat oven to 350°F. Wrap tortillas tightly in foil. Bake for about 10 minutes or until heated through.

egg and vegetable
SALAD WRAPS

Need an energy boost? High-protein eggs wrapped with crisp, refreshing veggies are the perfect solution. Enjoy these healthful sandwiches for lunch or a light supper.

Start to Finish: 35 minutes
Makes: 6 servings

- 6 **hard-cooked eggs, chopped**
- ½ **cup chopped cucumber**
- ½ **cup chopped yellow summer squash or zucchini**
- ¼ **cup shredded carrot**
- 2 **tablespoons chopped red onion**
- ¼ **cup mayonnaise or salad dressing**
- 2 **tablespoons Dijon-style mustard**
- 1 **tablespoon milk**
- 1 **teaspoon snipped fresh tarragon or basil, or ¼ teaspoon dried tarragon or basil, crushed**
- ¼ **teaspoon salt**
- ⅛ **teaspoon paprika**
- 6 **leaf lettuce leaves**
- 6 **6- to 7-inch whole wheat flour tortillas**
- 2 **roma tomatoes, thinly sliced**

1 In a large bowl, combine eggs, cucumber, squash, carrot, and red onion. For dressing, in a small bowl, stir together mayonnaise, Dijon mustard, milk, herb, salt, and paprika. Pour dressing over egg mixture; toss gently to coat.

2 For each sandwich, place a lettuce leaf on a tortilla. Place 3 or 4 tomato slices on top of the lettuce, slightly off center. Spoon about ½ cup of the egg mixture on top of the tomato slices. Roll up tortilla; secure with wooden pick, if necessary. Cut the tortilla rolls in half crosswise.

Nutrition facts per serving: 215 cal., 15 g total fat (3 g sat. fat), 218 mg chol., 427 mg sodium, 15 g carb., 9 g dietary fiber, 12 g protein.

cheese
AND EGGS

Oven Omelets with Pesto, *page 148*

fontina CHEESE AND ARTICHOKE PIZZA

Prep: 15 minutes
Bake: 13 minutes
Oven: 450°F
Makes: 6 servings

1   tablespoon olive oil or
    cooking oil

1   medium red onion, thinly
    sliced

2   cloves garlic, minced

1   12-inch Italian bread shell
    (such as Boboli brand)

1½ cups shredded fontina or
    Swiss cheese (6 ounces)

½   of a 9-ounce package
    frozen artichoke hearts,
    thawed and cut up

½   cup pitted kalamata
    olives, halved or
    quartered

    Coarsely ground black
    pepper

    Purchased Alfredo pasta
    sauce, warmed
    (optional)

1 Preheat oven to 450°F. In a medium skillet, heat oil over medium heat. Add onion and garlic; cook until tender and golden brown, stirring occasionally.

2 Place the bread shell on a lightly greased baking sheet. Bake for 5 minutes.

3 Sprinkle hot bread shell with ½ cup of the cheese. Arrange artichokes, olives, and cooked onion mixture on top of cheese. Sprinkle with the remaining cheese. Sprinkle lightly with pepper.

4 Bake for 8 to 10 minutes more or until cheese is melted and pizza is heated through. If desired, serve pizza with warm Alfredo sauce.

Nutrition facts per serving: 184 cal., 9 g total fat (3 g sat. fat), 19 mg chol., 390 mg sodium, 19 g carb., 1 g dietary fiber, 8 g protein.

salsa, BEAN, AND CHEESE PIZZA

Start to Finish: 20 minutes
Oven: 425°F
Makes: 4 servings

- 4   6-inch corn tortillas*
- 4   teaspoons olive oil
- 1   medium onion, chopped (½ cup)
- 1   fresh jalapeño chile pepper, seeded and finely chopped**
- 1   clove garlic, minced
- 1   cup canned black beans, rinsed and drained
- 1   cup chopped seeded tomato
- 4   ounces Monterey Jack, cheddar, or mozzarella cheese, shredded (1 cup)
- 2   tablespoons chopped fresh cilantro

1 Preheat oven to 425°F. Place tortillas on an ungreased baking sheet. Lightly brush tortillas on both sides with 1 teaspoon of the oil. Bake for about 3 minutes on each side, until lightly browned and crisp.

2 Meanwhile, in a large skillet, cook onion, chile pepper, and garlic in remaining 3 teaspoons oil over medium-high heat until onion is tender. Stir in black beans and tomato; heat through.

3 Sprinkle tortillas with half of the cheese. Spoon bean mixture over cheese. Sprinkle with remaining cheese. Bake for about 4 minutes or until cheese melts. Sprinkle with cilantro.

Nutrition facts per serving: 231 cal., 11 g total fat (4 g sat. fat), 20 mg chol., 496 mg sodium, 25 g carb., 6 g dietary fiber, 12 g protein.

*Tip: If you prefer, substitute purchased tostada shells for the corn tortillas. Reduce oil amount to 3 teaspoons and omit step 1.

**Tip: Because chile peppers contain volatile oils that can burn your skin and eyes, avoid direct contact with them as much as possible. When working with chile peppers, wear plastic or rubber gloves. If your bare hands do touch the peppers, wash your hands and nails well with soap and warm water.

southwestern BEAN AND CHEESE BAKE

Prep: 20 minutes
Bake: 45 minutes
Stand: 15 minutes
Oven: 325°F
Makes: 8 servings

1 **15-ounce can black beans, rinsed and drained**

¾ **cup canned enchilada sauce**

2 **4-ounce cans diced green chile peppers, drained**

½ **cup thinly sliced scallions**

Several dashes bottled hot pepper sauce (optional)

2 **cloves garlic, minced**

1 **cup shredded sharp cheddar cheese and/or shredded Monterey Jack cheese with jalapeño chile peppers (4 ounces)**

3 **egg whites**

3 **egg yolks**

2 **tablespoons all-purpose flour**

¼ **teaspoon salt**

½ **cup milk**

1 **tablespoon snipped fresh cilantro**

Sour cream (optional)

Fresh cilantro leaves (optional)

1 Preheat oven to 325°F. Grease a 2-quart square baking dish. In the prepared baking dish, combine black beans, enchilada sauce, green chile peppers, scallions, hot pepper sauce (if desired), and garlic. Sprinkle with cheese.

2 In a medium bowl, beat egg whites with an electric mixer on medium speed until soft peaks form (tips curl).

3 In a large bowl, combine egg yolks, flour, and salt. Using a wire whisk, beat mixture until combined (mixture will be stiff). Gradually whisk in milk until smooth. Fold the beaten egg whites and snipped cilantro into egg yolk mixture. Carefully pour the egg mixture over the bean mixture in baking dish.

4 Bake for about 45 minutes or until egg mixture appears set when gently shaken. Let stand for 15 minutes before serving. If desired, garnish with sour cream and cilantro leaves.

Nutrition facts per serving: 163 cal., 8 g total fat (4 g sat. fat), 96 mg chol., 488 mg sodium, 15 g carb., 4 g dietary fiber, 11 g protein.

cheese CALZONES

Prep: 50 minutes
Bake: 18 minutes
Oven: 375°F
Makes: 8 servings

1   16-ounce loaf frozen
    bread dough, thawed*
½   cup chopped onion
    (1 medium)
½   cup shredded carrot
    (1 medium)
½   cup shredded zucchini
2   cloves garlic, minced
1   egg, beaten
1   cup light ricotta cheese
1   cup shredded mozzarella
    cheese (4 ounces)
¼   cup grated Parmesan
    cheese
1   teaspoon dried Italian
    seasoning
    Grated Parmesan cheese
1   cup pizza or pasta sauce

1 Lightly coat a very large baking sheet with cooking spray; set aside. Divide bread dough into 8 equal pieces. Place dough on a lightly floured surface and cover with a towel. Let dough rest while preparing filling.

2 For filling, in a small saucepan cook onion, carrot, zucchini, and garlic, covered, in a small amount of boiling water for 3 minutes. Drain. In a medium bowl, stir together egg, ricotta cheese, mozzarella cheese, and ¼ cup Parmesan cheese. Add onion mixture and Italian seasoning.

3 Preheat oven to 375°F. Roll each piece of dough into a 6-inch circle. (If dough seems too elastic, let the dough rest for a few minutes; keep dough circles covered while rolling remaining dough circles.) Spread ⅓ cup filling over each circle, spreading to within ½ inch of edge. Moisten edges of dough with water. Fold each circle in half; seal edge with the tines of a fork. Prick tops with the fork; place calzones on prepared baking sheet. Brush tops with water and sprinkle with additional Parmesan.

4 Bake for 18 to 20 minutes or until golden. Meanwhile, in a small saucepan heat pizza sauce. Serve pizza sauce with calzones.

Nutrition facts per serving: 264 cal., 7 g total fat (3 g sat. fat), 43 mg chol., 503 mg sodium, 34 g carb., 2 g dietary fiber, 16 g protein.

*Tip: Plan ahead and thaw the dough overnight in your refrigerator.

skillet VEGETABLES ON CHEESE TOAST

Start to Finish: 20 minutes
Oven: broil
Makes: 4 servings

8 slices rustic wheat bread

2 tablespoons olive oil

½ of an 8-ounce package peeled fresh whole baby carrots, halved lengthwise

1 8-ounce package button mushrooms, halved

1 small red onion, cut into thin wedges

4 cloves garlic, peeled and coarsely chopped

2 tablespoons water

Salt and ground black pepper

4 ounces soft goat cheese

Olive oil (optional)

Fresh basil (optional)

1 Preheat broiler. Place bread on baking sheet; set aside.

2 In a large skillet, heat olive oil over medium-high heat. Add carrots, mushrooms, onion, and garlic; cook for 2 to 3 minutes or until vegetables just begin to brown. Add water. Cook, covered, over medium heat for about 5 minutes or until vegetables are crisp-tender, stirring once. Sprinkle with salt and pepper.

3 Meanwhile, for cheese toast, lightly toast bread 3 inches from boiler heat for 1 to 2 minutes. Spread goat cheese on one side of each slice. Broil 3 inches from heat for 1 to 2 minutes or until cheese is softened.

4 Place cheese toasts on plates; top with vegetables. If desired, drizzle with additional olive oil and sprinkle with basil.

Nutrition facts per serving: 461 cal., 21 g total fat (6 g sat. fat), 13 mg chol., 596 mg sodium, 56 g carb., 8 g dietary fiber, 15 g protein.

mock CHEESE SOUFFLÉ

Prep: 15 minutes
Chill: 2 to 24 hours
Bake: 45 minutes
Oven: 350°F
Makes: 6 servings

- **8 slices white bread, cubed (6 cups)**
- **1½ cups shredded sharp cheddar cheese or Monterey Jack cheese with jalapeño chile peppers**
- **4 eggs, lightly beaten**
- **1½ cups milk**
- **2 teaspoons vegetarian Worcestershire sauce**
- **½ teaspoon salt**

1 Place half of the bread cubes in ungreased 1½-quart soufflé dish. Top with half of the cheese. Repeat layers; press lightly.

2 In medium bowl, combine eggs, milk, vegetarian Worcestershire sauce, and salt. Pour mixture over layers in dish. Cover and chill for 2 to 24 hours.

3 Preheat oven to 350°F. Bake, uncovered, for 45 to 50 minutes or until a knife inserted near center comes out clean. Serve immediately.

Nutrition facts per serving: 284 cal., 15 g total fat (8 g sat. fat), 176 mg chol., 639 mg sodium, 21 g carb., 1 g dietary fiber, 16 g protein.

kale–goat cheese
FRITTATA

Start to Finish: 25 minutes
Oven: broil
Makes: 6 servings

2 cups coarsely torn
  fresh kale

1 medium onion, halved
  and thinly sliced

2 teaspoons olive oil

6 eggs

4 egg whites

¼ teaspoon salt

⅛ teaspoon ground black
  pepper

¼ cup drained oil-packed
  sun-dried tomatoes,
  thinly sliced

1 ounce goat cheese,
  crumbled

1 Preheat broiler. In 10-inch broilerproof skillet, cook and stir kale and onion in oil over medium heat for 10 minutes or until onion is tender.

2 Meanwhile, in medium bowl whisk together eggs, egg whites, salt, and pepper. Pour over kale mixture in skillet. Cook on medium-low heat. As egg mixture sets, run a spatula around the edge of the skillet, lifting egg mixture so the uncooked portion flows underneath. Continue cooking and lifting edge until egg mixture is almost set but still glossy and moist.

3 Sprinkle egg mixture with dried tomatoes and goat cheese. Broil 4 to 5 inches from the heat for 1 to 2 minutes or until eggs are set. Cut into wedges to serve.

Nutrition facts per serving: 145 cal., 9 g total fat (3 g sat. fat), 216 mg chol., 242 mg sodium, 6 g carb., 1 g dietary fiber, 11 g protein.

mediterranean FRITTATA

Start to Finish: 30 minutes
Oven: broil
Makes: 6 servings

3 **tablespoons olive oil**

1 **cup chopped onion**

1 **teaspoon bottled minced garlic**

8 **eggs**

¼ **cup half-and-half, light cream, or milk**

½ **cup crumbled feta cheese (2 ounces)**

½ **of a 7-ounce jar (½ cup) roasted red sweet peppers, drained and chopped**

½ **cup sliced kalamata or pitted black olives**

¼ **cup slivered fresh basil**

⅛ **teaspoon ground black pepper**

½ **cup onion-and-garlic croutons, coarsely crushed***

2 **tablespoons finely shredded Parmesan cheese**

1 Preheat broiler. In a 10-inch broilerproof skillet, heat 2 tablespoons of the oil over medium heat. Add onion and garlic; cook until onion is just tender.

2 Meanwhile, in a large bowl beat together eggs and half-and-half. Stir in feta cheese, sweet peppers, olives, basil, and black pepper. Pour over onion mixture in skillet. Cook over medium heat. As mixture sets, run a spatula around the edge of the skillet, lifting egg mixture to allow the uncooked portion to flow underneath. Continue cooking and lifting edges till egg mixture is almost set (surface will be moist). Reduce heat as necessary to prevent overcooking.

3 Combine crushed croutons, Parmesan cheese, and the remaining tablespoon of oil; sprinkle mixture over frittata. Broil 4 to 5 inches from heat for 1 to 2 minutes or until top is set. Cut frittata in wedges to serve.

Nutrition facts per serving: 242 cal., 19 g total fat (6 g sat. fat), 297 mg chol., 339 mg sodium, 7 g carb., 1 g dietary fiber, 12 g protein.

*Tip: Place the croutons in a resealable plastic bag and pound with a rolling pin to coarsely crush.

cheese AND MUSHROOM EGG CASSEROLE

Prep: 25 minutes
Bake: 20 minutes
Oven: 350°F
Makes: 10 servings

16 eggs

1 cup milk

2 tablespoons butter or margarine

3 cups sliced fresh mushrooms

½ cup thinly sliced scallions

1 10.75-ounce can condensed cream of broccoli or cream of asparagus soup

¼ cup milk

1 cup shredded Monterey Jack cheese (4 ounces)

¼ cup grated Parmesan cheese

1 Preheat oven to 350°F. In a large bowl, beat together eggs and the 1 cup milk with a rotary beater. In a 12-inch nonstick skillet, melt 1 tablespoon of the butter over medium heat. Add half of the egg mixture. Cook over medium heat, without stirring, until mixture begins to set on the bottom and around the edge.

2 Using a large spoon, lift and fold the partially cooked egg mixture so the uncooked portion flows underneath. Continue cooking until egg mixture is cooked through but is still glossy and moist. Remove from heat immediately.

3 Transfer scrambled eggs to a greased 3-quart rectangular baking dish. Scramble remaining eggs using remaining butter; remove from heat immediately. Transfer to the baking dish.

4 In the same nonstick skillet, cook mushrooms and scallions until tender. Stir in soup and the ¼ cup milk. Stir in Monterey Jack and Parmesan cheeses. Spread mixture over eggs in baking dish.

5 Bake, covered, for about 20 minutes or until heated through.

Nutrition facts per serving: 239 cal., 17 g total fat (8 g sat. fat), 361 mg chol., 435 mg sodium, 6 g carb., 1 g dietary fiber, 16 g protein.

poached EGGS WITH POLENTA AND BLACK BEANS

Start to Finish: 35 minutes
Makes: 4 servings

- 3 **medium roma tomatoes, seeded and chopped**
- ½ **cup canned black beans, rinsed and drained**
- 2 **tablespoons chopped red onion**
- 1 **fresh jalapeño chile pepper, seeded and finely chopped***
- 1 **tablespoon snipped fresh cilantro**
- 2 **teaspoons balsamic vinegar**
- 1 **teaspoon olive oil**
- ⅛ **teaspoon salt**
- ⅛ **teaspoon ground black pepper**
- 1 **16-ounce tube refrigerated plain cooked polenta**
- 1 **tablespoon olive oil**
- 4 **eggs**
- 2 **teaspoons snipped fresh cilantro**
- **Lime wedges**

1 For salsa, in a small bowl combine tomatoes, black beans, red onion, jalapeño chile, the 1 tablespoon cilantro, balsamic vinegar, the 1 teaspoon oil, salt, and black pepper. Set aside until ready to serve.

2 Unwrap the polenta and cut into 12 slices. In an extra-large nonstick skillet, heat the 1 tablespoon olive oil over medium heat. Add polenta; cook for 14 to 16 minutes or until polenta is browned, turning once halfway through cooking.

3 Meanwhile, to poach eggs, fill a large skillet half full with water. Bring to boiling; reduce heat to simmering (bubbles should begin to break the surface of the water). Break one of the eggs into a measuring cup. Carefully slide egg into simmering water, holding the lip of the cup as close to the water as possible. Repeat with the remaining eggs, allowing each egg an equal amount of space. Simmer, uncovered, for 3 to 5 minutes or until the egg whites are completely set and yolks begin to thicken but are not hard. Using a slotted spoon, remove eggs.

4 To serve, divide the polenta slices among plates. Top with the salsa and poached eggs. Sprinkle eggs with additional salt and black pepper. Sprinkle with the 2 teaspoons cilantro. Serve with lime wedges.

Nutrition facts per serving: 254 cal., 10 g total fat (2 g sat. fat), 213 mg chol., 768 mg sodium, 29 g carb., 6 g dietary fiber, 11 g protein

*Tip: Because chile peppers contain volatile oils that can burn your skin and eyes, avoid direct contact with them as much as possible. When working with chile peppers, wear plastic or rubber gloves. If your bare hands do touch the peppers, wash your hands and nails well with soap and warm water.

poached EGGS WITH GRAINY MUSTARD VINAIGRETTE

Start to Finish: 20 minutes
Makes: 4 servings

2   **tablespoons vinegar**

2   **tablespoons olive oil**

1   **tablespoon coarse brown mustard**

4   **large eggs**

8   **cups lightly packed torn fresh spinach sautéed in 1 tablespoon butter**

    Salt and ground black pepper

① In a small saucepan, combine vinegar, oil, and mustard. Bring to boiling over medium-high heat, stirring to combine. Reduce heat to low and keep warm, stirring again just before serving.

② Lightly grease 4 cups of an egg-poaching pan with oil. Place poacher cups over the pan of boiling water (water should not touch bottoms of cups); reduce heat to simmering. Break an egg into a measuring cup. Carefully slide egg into a poacher cup. Repeat with remaining eggs. Cover and cook for 4 to 5 minutes or until the whites are completely set and yolks begin to thicken but are not hard.

③ Run a knife around edges to loosen eggs. Arrange spinach on serving plates. Top with poached egg by inverting poaching cups. Top with grainy mustard vinaigrette. Season with salt and pepper.

Nutrition facts per serving: 179 cal., 15 g total fat (4 g sat. fat), 220 mg chol., 340 mg sodium, 3 g carb., 1 g dietary fiber, 8 g protein.

spring CRUSTLESS QUICHE

Prep: 25 minutes
Bake: 40 minutes
Cook: 10 minutes
Oven: 350°F
Makes: 6 to 8 servings

- 1 tablespoon butter
- 3 cups thickly sliced fresh mushrooms, such as cremini, shiitake, and/or portobello
- 1 clove garlic, minced
- 12 ounces asparagus spears
- 4 eggs, beaten
- 1½ cups whipping cream
- 2 teaspoons Dijon-style mustard
- ½ teaspoon salt
- ¼ teaspoon ground black pepper

 Pinch of ground red pepper
- 1 cup shredded Swiss or Emmenthal cheese

1 Preheat oven to 350°F. Lightly coat a 2-quart rectangular baking dish with cooking spray; set aside.

2 In a large skillet, melt butter over medium-high heat. Add mushrooms and garlic; cook and stir for 7 to 8 minutes or until tender and most of the liquid has evaporated. Remove from heat; set aside.

3 Snap off and discard woody bases from asparagus. If desired, scrape off scales. Cut asparagus into 1-inch pieces. Cook asparagus, covered, in a small amount of boiling lightly salted water for 3 to 5 minutes or until crisp-tender. Drain well, rinse with cold running water until cool; drain again.

4 In a large bowl, whisk together eggs, whipping cream, mustard, salt, black pepper, and ground red pepper. Stir in mushrooms, asparagus, and ½ cup of the cheese.

5 Pour mixture into prepared baking dish. Sprinkle evenly with remaining cheese. Bake, uncovered, for 40 to 45 minutes or until a knife inserted near the center comes out clean.

Nutrition facts per serving: 370 cal., 34 g total fat (19 g sat. fat), 246 mg chol., 361 mg sodium, 6 g carb., 1 g dietary fiber, 13 g protein.

oven OMELETS WITH PESTO

Start to Finish: 30 minutes
Oven: 400°F
Makes: 6 servings

- 12 **eggs**
- ¼ **cup water**
- ¾ **teaspoon salt**
- ⅛ **teaspoon ground black pepper**
- 1 **medium zucchini, halved lengthwise and thinly sliced**
- 1 **tablespoon olive oil**
  Spinach Pesto*
- 1 **medium roma tomato, seeded and chopped**
  Grated Parmesan cheese (optional)

1 Preheat oven to 400°F. Lightly coat a 15x10x1-inch baking pan with nonstick coating.

2 In a medium bowl, beat together eggs, water, salt, and pepper with a rotary beater until combined but not frothy. Place the prepared pan on an oven rack. Carefully pour the egg mixture into the pan. Bake for about 7 minutes or until egg mixture is set but still glossy.

3 Meanwhile, in a large skillet cook zucchini in hot oil until just tender. Remove from heat. Stir in about half of the Spinach Pesto.

4 Cut the omelet into six 5-inch squares. Using a large spatula, remove omelets and invert onto warm serving plates. Spoon zucchini mixture on half of each omelet; fold other half over filling, forming a triangle or a rectangle. Top with remaining pesto; sprinkle with chopped tomato and, if desired, Parmesan cheese.

***Spinach Pesto:** In a food processor, combine ½ cup packed torn fresh spinach; ¼ cup packed fresh basil leaves; 2 tablespoons grated Parmesan cheese; 1 small clove garlic, quartered; and pinch of salt. Cover and process with several on/off pulses until a paste forms, stopping the machine several times and scraping sides. With machine running, gradually add 1 tablespoon olive oil. Process until mixture is the consistency of soft butter.

Nutrition facts per serving: 202 cal., 15 g total fat (4 g sat. fat), 424 mg chol., 485 mg sodium, 3 g carb., 1 g dietary fiber, 14 g protein.

baked EGGS WITH CHEESE AND BASIL SAUCE

Prep: 15 minutes
Bake: 18 minutes
Oven: 350°F
Makes: 4 servings

3 **tablespoons butter or margarine**

2 **tablespoons all-purpose flour**

¼ **teaspoon salt**

⅛ **teaspoon ground black pepper**

3 **tablespoons snipped fresh basil, or ½ teaspoon dried basil, crushed**

1 **cup milk**

4 **eggs**

Salt and ground black pepper

¼ **cup shredded mozzarella cheese (1 ounce)**

Snipped fresh basil (optional)

1 Preheat oven to 350°F. For basil sauce, in a small saucepan melt butter over medium heat. Stir in flour, the ¼ teaspoon salt, the ⅛ teaspoon pepper, and, if using, the dried basil. Add milk all at once. Cook and stir until thickened and bubbly. Cook and stir for 1 minute more. Remove from heat. Stir in the 3 tablespoons fresh basil, if using.

2 Lightly coat four 8- to 10-ounce round baking dishes or 6-ounce custard cups with nonstick cooking spray. To assemble, spoon about 2 tablespoons of the basil sauce into each prepared dish. Gently break an egg into the center of each dish; season with salt and pepper. Spoon remaining basil sauce over eggs. Bake for 18 to 20 minutes or until eggs are set. Sprinkle with cheese. Let stand until cheese melts. If desired, garnish with additional snipped basil.

Nutrition facts per serving: 216 cal., 16 g total fat (9 g sat. fat), 245 mg chol., 419 mg sodium, 6 g carb., 0 g dietary fiber, 10 g protein.

grilled EGG SANDWICH

2 tablespoons mayonnaise or salad dressing

1 tablespoon Dijon-style mustard or brown mustard

4 slices English muffin bread or firm-textured white bread

2 tablespoons margarine or butter

4 eggs

4 to 6 spinach leaves

1 small tomato, sliced

2 slices Swiss or American cheese

2 tablespoons milk

1 In a small bowl, stir together mayonnaise and mustard. Spread the mustard mixture on one side of each bread slice. Set aside.

2 In a large skillet, melt 1 tablespoon of the margarine over medium heat. Break 2 of the eggs into skillet. Stir each egg gently with a fork to break up yolk. Cook for 3 to 4 minutes or until eggs are desired doneness, turning once.

3 Place each egg on mustard side of a bread slice. Layer the spinach, tomato, and cheese on eggs. Top with the remaining bread slices, mustard sides down.

4 In a shallow dish, beat together the remaining 2 eggs and the milk. Carefully dip sandwiches in egg mixture, coating both sides. In the same skillet, melt the remaining 1 tablespoon margarine over medium heat. Add sandwiches; cook for about 4 minutes or until bread is golden brown, turning once.

Nutrition facts per serving: 595 cal., 42 g total fat (11 g sat. fat), 454 mg chol., 692 mg sodium, 31 g carb., 1 g dietary fiber, 24 g protein.

baked BREAKFAST PORTOBELLOS

Prep: 15 minutes
Bake: 15 minutes
Oven: 350°F
Makes: 4 servings

- **4 fresh portobello mushrooms (3 to 5 ounces each)**
- **4 eggs**
- **3 tablespoons water**
- **⅛ teaspoon salt**
- **Pinch of ground black pepper**
- **2 tablespoons sliced scallion**
- **2 tablespoons chopped bottled roasted red sweet peppers, drained**

1 Preheat oven to 350°F. Clean and remove stems from mushrooms. Place mushroom caps, stem side up, in an ungreased shallow baking pan. Bake, uncovered, for 15 to 20 minutes or until tender.

2 Meanwhile, in a medium bowl whisk together eggs, water, salt, and pepper. Lightly coat a large nonstick skillet with cooking spray. Heat skillet over medium heat. Add scallion to skillet; cook and stir for 30 seconds. Pour egg mixture into skillet. Cook, without stirring, until mixture begins to set on the bottom and around edge.

3 With a spatula or a large spoon, lift and fold partially cooked egg mixture so that the uncooked portion flows underneath. Continue cooking over medium heat for 2 to 3 minutes or until egg mixture is cooked through but is still glossy and moist. Remove from heat.

4 Fill mushrooms with scrambled eggs. Top with roasted peppers.

Nutrition facts per serving: 106 cal., 5 g total fat (2 g sat. fat), 213 mg chol., 143 mg sodium, 7 g carb., 2 g dietary fiber, 9 g protein.

beans, RICE, AND GRAINS

**Risotto with Beans and
Vegetables,** *page 172*

polenta AND BLACK BEANS

Start to Finish: 25 minutes
Makes: 4 servings

3 cups water

1 cup yellow cornmeal*

1 cup water

½ teaspoon salt

1 15-ounce can black beans, rinsed and drained

1 14.5-ounce can diced tomatoes, undrained

1 cup bottled salsa with cilantro or other salsa

¾ cup shredded Mexican cheese blend (3 ounces)

1 For polenta, in a large saucepan bring the 3 cups water to boiling. In a medium bowl, combine cornmeal, the 1 cup water, and ½ teaspoon salt. Stir cornmeal mixture slowly into the boiling water. Cook and stir until mixture comes to boiling. Reduce heat to low. Cook for 5 to 10 minutes or until mixture is thick, stirring occasionally. (If mixture is too thick, stir in additional water.)

2 Meanwhile, in a large skillet combine the beans, tomatoes, and salsa. Bring mixture to boiling; reduce heat. Simmer, uncovered, for 10 minutes, stirring frequently. Stir ½ cup of the cheese into the polenta. Divide polenta among shallow bowls. Top with the bean mixture and sprinkle with the remaining cheese.

Nutrition facts per serving: 311 cal., 8 g total fat (4 g sat. fat), 19 mg chol., 751 mg sodium, 49 g carb., 8 g dietary fiber, 15 g protein.

*Tip: Polenta can be made from a variety of cornmeal products. In this recipe, yellow cornmeal produces the best results.

spicy BLACK BEANS AND RICE

Prep: 5 minutes
Cook: 20 minutes
Makes: 4 servings

- ½ **cup chopped onion (1 medium)**
- 4 **cloves garlic, minced**
- 2 **tablespoons olive oil or cooking oil**
- 1 **15-ounce can black beans, rinsed and drained**
- 1 **14.5-ounce can Mexican-style stewed tomatoes**
- ½ **cup salsa**
- ¼ **teaspoon salt**
- ⅛ **to ¼ teaspoon cayenne pepper**
- 2 **cups hot cooked brown or long grain rice**
- ½ **cup shredded cheddar cheese, Monterey Jack cheese, or Mexican cheese blend (optional)**
- ¼ **cup chopped onion (optional)**

1 In a medium saucepan, cook the ½ cup onion and garlic in hot oil until tender but not brown. Carefully stir in beans, undrained tomatoes, salsa, salt, and cayenne pepper. Bring to boiling; reduce heat. Simmer, uncovered, for 15 minutes.

2 To serve, mound rice on serving plates; make a well in each mound. Spoon the black bean mixture into wells. If desired, sprinkle with shredded cheese and the ¼ cup chopped onion.

Nutrition facts per serving: 284 cal., 8 g total fat (1 g sat. fat), 0 mg chol., 835 mg sodium, 48 g carb., 7 g dietary fiber, 11 g protein.

black BEAN CAKES WITH SALSA

A corn muffin mix provides the base for these Mexican-style black bean cakes topped with chili-spiked sour cream.

Start to Finish: 25 minutes
Makes: 4 (2-cake) servings

1½ cups prepared salsa

1 jalapeño chile pepper

2 15-ounce cans black beans, rinsed and drained

1 8.5-ounce package corn muffin mix

3 teaspoons chili powder

2 tablespoons olive oil

½ cup sour cream

1 In a colander, drain ½ cup of the salsa. Seed and finely chop half of the jalapeño;* thinly slice remaining half. In a large bowl, mash beans with vegetable masher or fork. Stir in muffin mix, drained salsa, 2½ teaspoons of the chili powder, and the chopped jalapeño.

2 In an extra-large skillet, heat 1 tablespoon of the olive oil over medium-high heat. Add four ½-cup mounds bean mixture to skillet. Flatten mounds with spatula to 3½-inch round cakes. Cook for about 3 minutes on each side or until browned. Remove from skillet. Repeat with remaining olive oil and bean mixture.

3 In a small bowl, combine sour cream and remaining ½ teaspoon chili powder. Top cakes with remaining salsa, sliced jalapeño, and seasoned sour cream.

Nutrition facts per serving: 519 cal., 19 g total fat (4 g sat. fat), 11 mg chol., 1553 mg sodium, 79 g carb., 12 g dietary fiber, 20 g protein.

*Tip: Because chile peppers contain volatile oils that can burn your skin and eyes, avoid direct contact with them as much as possible. When working with chile peppers, wear plastic or rubber gloves. If your bare hands do touch the peppers, wash your hands and nails well with soap and warm water.

chili bean–stuffed PEPPERS

This zesty slow cooker recipe will add a spicy kick to your everyday dinner menu.

Prep: 30 minutes
Cook: 6 to 6½ hours (low)
or 3 to 3½ hours
(high)
Makes: 4 servings

4 **small to medium green, red, or yellow sweet peppers**

1 **cup cooked converted rice**

1 **15-ounce can chili beans with chili gravy**

1 **15-ounce can or two 8-ounce cans no-salt-added tomato sauce**

⅓ **cup finely chopped onion**

3 **ounces Monterey Jack cheese, shredded (¾ cup)**

1 Remove tops, membranes, and seeds from sweet peppers. Chop enough tops to make ⅓ cup. If necessary, cut a thin slice from the bottom of each pepper so they sit flat. In a medium bowl, stir together rice and undrained beans; spoon into peppers. Pour tomato sauce into the bottom of a 4½-, 5-, or 6-quart slow cooker; stir in reserved chopped pepper and onion. Place peppers, filled side up, in cooker.

2 Cover and cook on low-heat setting for 6 to 6½ hours or on high-heat setting for 3 to 3½ hours.

3 To serve, transfer peppers to serving plate and cut in half, if desired. Spoon tomato sauce over peppers and sprinkle with cheese.

Nutrition facts per serving: 283 cal., 8 g total fat (4 g sat. fat), 19 mg chol., 407 mg sodium, 40 g carb., 9 g dietary fiber, 15 g protein.

meatless SHEPHERD'S PIE

The mix of white kidney beans and soybeans provides lots of protein for this potato-topped one-dish meal.

Prep: 25 minutes
Cook: 10 to 12 hours
(low) or 5 to
6 hours (high)
Makes: 8 servings

2 **19-ounce cans white kidney beans (cannellini beans), rinsed and drained**

1 **12-ounce package frozen sweet soybeans (edamame)**

3 **carrots, peeled and sliced**

1 **large onion, cut into wedges**

1 **14.5-ounce can diced tomatoes, drained**

1 **12-ounce jar mushroom gravy**

2 **cloves garlic, minced**

1 **24-ounce package refrigerated mashed potatoes**

1 **cup shredded cheddar cheese (4 ounces)**

1 In a 5- to 6-quart slow cooker, stir together white kidney beans, soybeans, carrots, onion, tomatoes, gravy, and garlic.

2 Cover and cook on low-heat setting for 10 to 12 hours or on high-heat setting for 5 to 6 hours.

3 If using low-heat setting, turn to high-heat setting. Spoon mashed potatoes on top of bean mixture. Sprinkle with cheese. Cover and cook for about 30 minutes more or until potatoes are heated through.

Nutrition facts per serving: 320 cal., 9 g total fat (3 g sat. fat), 15 mg chol., 805 mg sodium, 47 g carb., 13 g dietary fiber, 20 g protein.

beans, BARLEY, AND TOMATOES

Start to Finish: 30 minutes
Makes: 4 servings

- 1 14-ounce can vegetable broth
- 1 teaspoon Greek seasoning or garam masala
- 1 cup frozen sweet soybeans (edamame)
- ¾ cup quick-cooking barley
- ½ cup packaged shredded carrot (1 medium)
- 4 cups packaged fresh spinach leaves
- 4 small to medium tomatoes, sliced

1 In a medium saucepan, bring broth and seasoning to boiling. Add soybeans and barley. Return to boiling; reduce heat. Simmer, covered, for 12 minutes. Stir carrot into barley mixture.

2 Meanwhile, arrange spinach on salad plates; top with tomato slices. Using a slotted spoon, spoon barley mixture over tomatoes (or drain barley mixture; spoon over tomato slices).

Nutrition facts per serving: 171 cal., 3 g total fat (0 g sat. fat), 0 mg chol., 484 mg sodium, 33 g carb., 10 g dietary fiber, 9 g protein.

bean BURRITOS

Tart and tangy lime makes these burritos pop with flavor, but you can easily leave out the zest and substitute bottled lime or lemon juice for the fresh.

Start to Finish: 20 minutes
Makes: 4 burritos

4 9- to 10-inch flour tortillas

1 16-ounce can refried beans

¼ cup purchased salsa

¼ cup mayonnaise

½ teaspoon finely shredded lime zest

1 tablespoon lime juice

2 cups shredded leaf or iceberg lettuce

½ cup seeded (if desired) and chopped tomato (1 medium)

½ cup shredded Monterey Jack cheese (2 ounces)

1️⃣ Place tortillas between microwave-safe paper towels. Microwave on 100% power (high) for 20 to 30 seconds or until warm.

2️⃣ Meanwhile, in a small saucepan combine refried beans and salsa. Cook over medium heat until heated through, stirring frequently.

3️⃣ In a medium bowl, combine mayonnaise, lime zest, and lime juice. Add lettuce and tomato; toss gently to coat.

4️⃣ Spoon about ½ cup of the bean mixture onto each tortilla just below the center. Top each with 2 tablespoons of the cheese and about ⅓ cup of the lettuce mixture. Fold bottom edge of each tortilla up and over filling. Fold in opposite sides; roll up from the bottom.

Nutrition facts per burrito: 414 cal., 19 g total fat (6 g sat. fat), 29 mg chol., 992 mg sodium, 47 g carb., 9 g dietary fiber, 15 g protein.

tex-mex BEANS WITH CORNMEAL DUMPLINGS

Start to Finish: 35 minutes
Makes: 5 servings

1 cup chopped onion
  (1 large)
¾ cup water
1 clove garlic, minced
2 8-ounce cans no-salt-
  added tomato sauce
1 15-ounce can garbanzo
  beans (chickpeas), rinsed
  and drained
1 15-ounce can red kidney
  beans, rinsed and
  drained
1 4-ounce can diced green
  chile peppers, drained
2 teaspoons chili powder
¼ teaspoon salt
1½ teaspoons cornstarch
1 tablespoon cold water
  Cornmeal Dumplings*

1. In a large skillet, combine onion, the ¾ cup water, and garlic. Bring to boiling; reduce heat. Simmer, covered, for about 5 minutes or until onion is tender. Stir in tomato sauce, drained beans, drained chile peppers, chili powder, and salt.

2. In a small bowl, stir together cornstarch and the 1 tablespoon cold water; stir into bean mixture. Cook and stir until slightly thickened and bubbly. Reduce heat.

3. Using two spoons, drop Cornmeal Dumplings dough into 10 mounds on top of hot bean mixture.

4. Cover and simmer for 10 to 12 minutes or until a toothpick inserted into the center of a dumpling comes out clean. (Do not lift cover during cooking.)

*Cornmeal Dumplings: In a medium bowl, stir together ⅓ cup all-purpose flour, ⅓ cup yellow cornmeal, 1 teaspoon baking powder, and ¼ teaspoon salt. In a small bowl, combine 1 egg white, ¼ cup fat-free milk, and 2 tablespoons vegetable oil. Add milk mixture to cornmeal mixture; stir just until combined.

Nutrition facts per serving: 350 cal., 7 g total fat (1 g sat. fat), 0 mg chol., 803 mg sodium, 61 g carb., 12 g dietary fiber, 15 g protein.

red BEANS CREOLE

Prep: 25 minutes
Stand: 1 hour
Cook: 11 to 13 hours
    (low) or 5½ hours
    to 6½ hours (high)
Makes: 4 or 5 servings

3½ **cups dried red beans
   (1½ pounds), rinsed
   and drained**

 5 **cups water**

 3 **cups chopped onions
   (3 large)**

 2 **4-ounce cans (drained
   weight) sliced
   mushrooms, drained**

 6 **cloves garlic, minced**

 2 **tablespoons Creole
   seasoning**

 1 **14.5-ounce can diced
   tomatoes with garlic,
   basil, and oregano**

 2 **cups instant brown rice**

 2 **medium green sweet
   peppers, cut into strips**

   **Bottled hot pepper sauce
   (optional)**

1 Place beans in a large saucepan. Add enough water to cover beans by 2 inches. Bring to boiling; reduce heat. Simmer, uncovered, for 10 minutes. Remove from heat. Cover and let stand for 1 hour. Drain and rinse beans.

2 In a 3½- or 4-quart slow cooker, combine beans, the 5 cups water, the onion, mushrooms, garlic, and Creole seasoning.

3 Cover and cook on low-heat setting for 11 to 13 hours or on high-heat setting for 5½ to 6½ hours.

4 If using low-heat setting, turn to high-heat setting. Stir in undrained tomatoes, uncooked rice, and sweet peppers. Cover and cook for 30 minutes more. If desired, serve with bottled hot pepper sauce.

Nutrition facts per serving: 415 cal., 2 g total fat (0 g sat. fat), 0 mg chol., 541 mg sodium, 81 g carb., 16 g dietary fiber, 23 g protein.

italian THREE-BEAN AND RICE SKILLET

Red beans, lima beans, and green beans are a tasty trio in this basil-accented skillet meal.

Prep: 15 minutes
Cook: 15 minutes
Makes: 4 servings

- 1 **15- to 15.5-ounce can small red beans or red kidney beans, rinsed and drained**
- 1 **14.5-ounce can Italian-style stewed tomatoes**
- 1 **cup vegetable broth**
- ¾ **cup quick-cooking brown rice**
- ½ **of a 10-ounce package frozen baby lima beans**
- ½ **of a 9-ounce package frozen cut green beans**
- ½ **teaspoon dried basil, crushed, or dried Italian seasoning, crushed**
- 1 **cup spaghetti sauce**
- 2 **ounces thinly sliced mozzarella cheese, or ¼ cup grated Parmesan cheese (optional)**

1 In a large skillet, combine red beans, undrained tomatoes, broth, rice, lima beans, green beans, and dried seasoning. Bring to boiling; reduce heat. Cover and simmer for about 15 minutes or until rice is tender.

2 Stir in spaghetti sauce. Heat through. If desired, top with mozzarella or Parmesan cheese.

Nutrition facts per serving: 259 cal., 4 g total fat (0 g sat. fat), 0 mg chol., 1103 mg sodium, 50 g carb., 10 g dietary fiber, 14 g protein.

fried RICE

Start to Finish: 30 minutes
Makes: 4 servings

4 **eggs, lightly beaten**

2 **teaspoons soy sauce**

2 **teaspoons vegetable oil**

2 **cloves garlic, minced**

2 **tablespoons vegetable oil**

1 **cup thinly bias-sliced celery (2 stalks)**

1½ **cups sliced fresh mushrooms (4 ounces)**

4 **cups chilled cooked white rice**

1 **cup thin bite-size strips carrots (2 medium)**

1 **cup frozen peas**

¼ **cup soy sauce**

½ **cup sliced scallions**

1 In a small bowl, combine eggs and the 2 teaspoons soy sauce.

2 Pour the 2 teaspoons oil into a wok or large skillet; heat wok over medium heat. Add garlic; cook and stir for 30 seconds. Add egg mixture. Cook, without stirring, until mixture begins to set on the bottom and around the edge. Using a spatula or large spoon, lift and fold the partially cooked egg mixture so that the uncooked portion flows underneath. Continue cooking for 2 to 3 minutes or until egg mixture is cooked through but is still glossy and moist. Remove wok from heat. Remove egg mixture from wok. Cut up any large pieces of egg mixture.

3 Pour the 2 tablespoons oil into wok or skillet; heat wok over medium-high heat. (Add more oil as necessary during cooking.) Add celery; cook and stir for 1 minute. Add mushrooms; cook and stir for 1 to 2 minutes or until vegetables are crisp-tender.

4 Add cooked rice, carrots, and peas. Sprinkle with the ¼ cup soy sauce. Cook and stir for 4 to 6 minutes or until heated through. Add cooked egg mixture and scallions. Cook and stir for about 1 minute more or until heated through.

Nutrition facts per serving: 416 cal., 16 g total fat (2 g sat. fat), 212 mg chol., 1229 mg sodium, 52 g carb., 5 g dietary fiber, 17 g protein.

lentil- and rice-stuffed
PEPPERS

Prep: 30 minutes
Cook: 3 to 3½ hours (high)
Makes: 8 servings

1½ **cups chopped carrots**

1½ **cups chopped celery**

1 **cup dried brown lentils, rinsed and drained**

⅔ **cup brown rice**

2 **tablespoons packed brown sugar**

2 **tablespoons yellow mustard**

½ **teaspoon salt**

2 **14-ounce cans vegetable broth**

½ **cup water**

1 **15-ounce can tomato sauce with garlic and onion**

2 **tablespoons cider vinegar**

4 **green and/or red sweet peppers**

Snipped fresh flat-leaf parsley (optional)

1 In a 3½- or 4-quart slow cooker, combine carrots, celery, lentils, uncooked brown rice, brown sugar, mustard, and salt. Stir in vegetable broth and the water.

2 Cover and cook on high-heat setting for 3 to 3½ hours. Stir in tomato sauce and vinegar. Cover and cook for 30 minutes more.

3 Halve sweet peppers lengthwise; remove seeds and membranes.* To serve, spoon lentil mixture in and around pepper halves. If desired, sprinkle with parsley.

Nutrition facts per serving: 206 cal., 1 g total fat (0 g sat. fat), 0 mg chol., 848 mg sodium, 40 g carb., 10 g dietary fiber, 9 g protein.

*Tip: If desired, in a Dutch oven cook sweet pepper halves in a large amount of boiling water for about 3 minutes or until crisp-tender. Drain well.

risotto WITH BEANS AND VEGETABLES

Start to Finish: 30 minutes
Makes: 4 servings

3 cups vegetable broth

2 cups sliced fresh
  mushrooms

½ cup chopped onion
  (1 medium)

2 cloves garlic, minced

2 tablespoons olive oil

1 cup arborio rice

1 cup finely chopped
  zucchini (1 small)

1 cup finely chopped
  carrots (2 medium)

1 15-ounce can cannellini
  beans (white kidney
  beans) or pinto beans,
  rinsed and drained

½ cup finely shredded
  Parmesan cheese

2 tablespoons snipped
  fresh Italian (flat-leaf)
  parsley

  Finely shredded Parmesan
  cheese (optional)

1 In a medium saucepan, bring broth to boiling; reduce heat. Simmer until needed. Meanwhile, in a large saucepan cook mushrooms, onion, and garlic in hot oil over medium heat for about 5 minutes or until onion is tender. Add uncooked rice. Cook and stir for about 5 minutes more or until rice is golden brown.

2 Slowly add 1 cup of the broth to rice mixture, stirring constantly. Continue to cook and stir until liquid is absorbed. Add another ½ cup of the broth, the zucchini, and carrots to rice mixture, stirring constantly. Continue to cook and stir until liquid is absorbed. Add another 1 cup broth, ½ cup at a time, stirring constantly until broth is absorbed. (This should take about 20 minutes.)

3 Stir the remaining ½ cup broth into rice mixture. Cook and stir until rice is slightly creamy and just tender. Stir in beans and the ½ cup Parmesan cheese; heat through. Sprinkle with parsley and, if desired, additional Parmesan cheese.

Nutrition facts per serving: 340 cal., 11 g total fat (3 g sat. fat), 9 mg chol., 1074 mg sodium, 53 g carb., 7 g dietary fiber, 15 g protein.

brown RICE PRIMAVERA

Flecks of colorful zucchini, sweet peppers, and tomatoes dress up the brown rice in this one-dish meal. The addition of feta cheese at the end lends a tangy note.

Prep: 20 minutes
Cook: 2 to 2½ hours (high)
Makes: 6 servings

1 **medium eggplant (about 1 pound), peeled if desired and cubed**

2 **medium zucchini, halved lengthwise and cut into ½-inch pieces (2½ cups)**

1 **medium onion, cut into thin wedges**

1 **14-ounce can vegetable broth**

2 **medium red and/or yellow sweet peppers, cut into thin bite-size strips**

1 **14.5-ounce can diced tomatoes with garlic, basil, and oregano, drained**

1 **cup instant brown rice**

2 **cups crumbled feta cheese (8 ounces)**

1 In a 5- to 6-quart slow cooker, combine eggplant, zucchini, and onion. Pour broth over mixture in cooker. Cover and cook on high-heat setting (do not use low-heat setting) for 2 to 2½ hours.

2 Stir in sweet pepper, tomatoes, and uncooked brown rice. Cover and cook for 30 minutes more. Sprinkle individual servings with feta cheese.

Nutrition facts per serving: 212 cal., 9 g total fat (6 g sat. fat), 34 mg chol., 1045 mg sodium, 26 g carb., 5 g dietary fiber, 9 g protein.

brown rice–spinach
CUSTARDS

Prep: 25 minutes
Bake: 25 minutes
Oven: 350°F
Makes: 6 servings

1 tablespoon olive oil

1 medium onion, chopped

4 eggs

½ cup low-fat cottage cheese

3 ounces reduced-fat feta cheese, crumbled

1 tablespoon snipped fresh dill, or ½ teaspoon dried dill

½ teaspoon salt

2 10-ounce packages frozen chopped spinach, thawed and well drained

2 cups cooked brown rice

1 tablespoon lemon juice

Fresh lemon zest strips (optional)

1 Preheat oven to 350°F. In a small skillet, heat oil over medium heat. Add onion; cook until tender, stirring occasionally. Cool slightly.

2 In a large bowl, beat eggs with a fork. Stir in cottage cheese, feta cheese, dill, salt, and cooked onion. Add spinach, brown rice, and lemon juice, stirring until well mixed. Place six 8- to 10-ounce ramekins or custard cups in a 15x10x1-inch baking pan. Divide rice mixture among the dishes. Bake for 25 to 30 minutes or until a knife inserted near the center of each custard comes out clean. If desired, garnish with lemon zest.

Nutrition facts per serving: 213 cal., 8 g total fat (3 g sat. fat), 146 mg chol., 648 mg sodium, 20 g carb., 4 g dietary fiber, 14 g protein.

grain-vegetable MEDLEY

Prep: 20 minutes
Cook: 10 minutes
Stand: 5 minutes
Makes: 4 (about 1-cup) servings

1 **14-ounce can reduced-sodium chicken broth**

¼ **cup water**

1½ **cups fresh green beans, trimmed and cut into 2-inch-long pieces**

⅔ **cup quick-cooking barley**

2 **tablespoons lemon juice**

1 **tablespoon olive oil**

⅛ **teaspoon salt**

⅛ **teaspoon ground black pepper**

½ **cup whole wheat couscous**

4 **cups coarsely shredded fresh spinach**

¼ **cup sliced scallions**

1½ **teaspoons snipped fresh thyme or ½ teaspoon dried thyme, crushed**

Lemon wedges (optional)

1 In a large saucepan bring chicken broth and the water to boiling; stir in green beans and uncooked barley. Return to boiling; reduce heat. Cover and simmer for 10 to 12 minutes or until barley is tender.

2 Meanwhile, in a small bowl whisk together lemon juice, oil, salt, and pepper.

3 Stir uncooked couscous into barley mixture. Stir in lemon juice mixture, spinach, green onions, and thyme. Remove from heat. Cover and let stand for 5 minutes. To serve, fluff with a fork. If desired, serve with lemon wedges.

Nutrition facts per serving: 274 cal., 5 g total fat (1 g sat. fat), 0 mg chol., 340 mg sodium, 51 g carb., 11 g dietary fiber, 11 g protein.

multigrain PILAF

Three kinds of grains make this dish wholesome, filling, and infinitely interesting.

Prep: 25 minutes
Cook: 6 to 8 hours (low)
     or 3 to 4 hours
     (high)
Makes: 6 servings

⅔ **cup wheat berries**

½ **cup regular barley**

½ **cup wild rice**

2 **14-ounce cans vegetable broth**

2 **cups frozen sweet soybeans (edamame) or baby lima beans**

1 **medium red sweet pepper, chopped**

1 **medium onion, finely chopped**

1 **tablespoon butter or margarine**

¾ **teaspoon dried sage, crushed**

½ **teaspoon salt**

¼ **teaspoon coarsely ground black pepper**

4 **cloves garlic, minced**
   Grated Parmesan cheese (optional)

1 Rinse and drain wheat berries, barley, and wild rice. In a 3½- or 4-quart slow cooker, combine wheat berries, barley, wild rice, vegetable broth, soybeans, sweet pepper, onion, butter, sage, salt, black pepper, and garlic.

2 Cover and cook on low-heat setting for 6 to 8 hours or on high-heat setting for 3 to 4 hours. Stir before serving. If desired, sprinkle each serving with Parmesan cheese.

Nutrition facts per serving: 342 cal., 9 g total fat (2 g sat. fat), 5 mg chol., 814 mg sodium, 50 g carb., 10 g dietary fiber, 20 g protein.

risotto-style BARLEY AND VEGETABLES

No doubt about it—a vegetable risotto is a great vegetarian main-dish mainstay. Here, the concept takes an unexpected turn, with a delightfully nutty barley base.

Start to Finish: 30 minutes
Makes: 4 servings

- ⅔ **cup thinly sliced zucchini**
- ⅓ **cup chopped onion**
- ⅓ **cup chopped carrot**
- ¼ **teaspoon dried rosemary, crushed**
- ⅛ **teaspoon ground black pepper**
- 1 **tablespoon olive oil or cooking oil**
- ⅔ **cup quick-cooking barley**
- 1 **14.5-ounce can vegetable broth**
- ¼ **cup evaporated milk, half-and-half, or light cream**
  Salt

1. In a medium saucepan, cook and stir the zucchini, onion, carrot, rosemary, and black pepper in hot oil just until vegetables are tender. Stir in barley.

2. Meanwhile, in a small saucepan bring vegetable broth to boiling. Reduce heat and simmer. Slowly add 1 cup of the broth to barley mixture, stirring constantly. Continue to cook and stir over medium heat until liquid is absorbed. Add the remaining broth, about ½ cup at a time, stirring constantly until liquid is absorbed. (This should take 10 to 15 minutes total.)

3. Stir in evaporated milk. Cook and stir for 2 minutes more. Season to taste with salt and additional black pepper.

Nutrition facts per serving: 155 cal., 6 g total fat (1 g sat. fat), 5 mg chol., 244 mg sodium, 23 g carb., 3 g dietary fiber, 4 g protein.

pasta

Artichoke-Basil Lasagna, *page 183*

black bean LASAGNA

This south-of-the-border-style vegetarian casserole is loaded with plenty of flavor.

Prep: 45 minutes
Bake: 35 minutes
Stand: 10 minutes
Oven: 350°F
Makes: 8 servings

9 **lasagna noodles**

2 **15-ounce cans black beans, rinsed and drained**

1 **egg, lightly beaten**

1 **12-ounce container cottage cheese**

1 **8-ounce package cream cheese, cut into cubes and softened**

1½ **cups shredded Monterey Jack cheese**

1 **cup chopped onion**

¾ **cup chopped green sweet pepper**

2 **cloves garlic, minced**

1 **tablespoon cooking oil**

1 **15-ounce can Italian-style tomato sauce**

4 **teaspoons dried cilantro, crushed**

1 **teaspoon ground cumin**

Coarsely chopped tomatoes

1 Cook lasagna noodles according to package directions; drain. Rinse noodles with cold water; drain well. Set aside. In a small bowl, mash one can of the beans with a potato masher. In a medium bowl, combine egg, cottage cheese, cream cheese, and 1 cup of the Monterey Jack cheese; set aside.

2 In a large skillet, cook onion, sweet pepper, and garlic in hot oil over medium-high heat until tender. Stir in mashed beans, the remaining can of whole beans, tomato sauce, cilantro, and cumin; heat through.

3 Preheat oven to 350°F. Arrange 3 of the noodles in a lightly greased 3-quart rectangular baking dish. Top with one-third (about 1⅓ cups) of the bean mixture. Spoon half (about 1 cup) of the cheese mixture over bean mixture. Repeat layers. Top with remaining noodles and bean mixture.

4 Bake, covered, for 35 to 40 minutes or until heated through. Sprinkle with the remaining ½ cup Monterey Jack cheese. Let stand for 10 minutes before serving. Garnish with chopped tomatoes.

Nutrition facts per serving: 456 cal., 22 g total fat (12 g sat. fat), 83 mg chol., 857 mg sodium, 46 g carb., 8 g dietary fiber, 25 g protein.

artichoke-basil LASAGNA

Prep: 45 minutes
Bake: 40 minutes
Stand: 15 minutes
Oven: 350°F
Makes: 8 servings

9 whole grain lasagna noodles

1 tablespoon olive oil

2 8- or 9-ounce packages frozen artichoke hearts, thawed and well drained

¼ cup pine nuts

4 cloves garlic, minced

1 15-ounce carton light ricotta cheese

1½ cups reduced-fat shredded Italian blend cheese or part-skim mozzarella cheese (6 ounces)

1 cup snipped fresh basil, or 4 teaspoons dried basil, crushed

1 egg

¼ teaspoon salt

1 cup chicken-flavored vegetable broth

¼ cup all-purpose flour

2 cups fat-free milk

   Chopped fresh tomato (optional)

   Snipped fresh parsley (optional)

1 Preheat oven to 350°F. Cook pasta according to package directions; drain in colander. Rinse with cold water; drain again. Place noodles in a single layer on a sheet of foil; set aside.

2 In a large skillet, heat oil over medium heat. Add artichokes, pine nuts, and garlic; cook for about 5 minutes or until artichokes, nuts, and garlic start to brown, stirring frequently. Transfer to a large bowl.

3 Add ricotta cheese, ½ cup of the Italian blend cheese, ½ cup of the fresh basil or 1 tablespoon of the dried basil, the egg, and salt; stir to combine.

4 For sauce, in a medium saucepan whisk together broth and flour until smooth. Stir in milk. Cook and stir over medium heat until sauce is slightly thickened and bubbly. Remove from heat. Stir in the remaining ½ cup fresh basil or 1 teaspoon dried basil.

5 Spread 1 cup of the sauce in the bottom of a 3-quart rectangular baking dish. Top with one-third of the cooked lasagna noodles. Spread with one-third of the ricotta mixture, then one-third of the remaining sauce. Sprinkle with ⅓ cup of the remaining Italian blend cheese. Repeat layers twice, beginning with the lasagna noodles and ending with the Italian blend cheese.

6 Bake, uncovered, for about 40 minutes or until heated through and top is lightly brown. Let stand for 15 minutes before serving. If desired, top with tomato and parsley.

Nutrition facts per serving: 329 cal., 12 g total fat (5 g sat. fat), 52 mg chol., 443 mg sodium, 35 g carb., 7 g dietary fiber, 21 g protein.

cheese MANICOTTI WITH ROASTED PEPPER SAUCE

Prep: 30 minutes
Bake: 25 minutes
Stand: 10 minutes
Oven: 350°F
Makes: 4 servings

8 manicotti shells

1 cup chopped fresh mushrooms

¾ cup shredded carrot

3 or 4 cloves garlic, minced

1 cup light ricotta cheese or low-fat cream-style cottage cheese

¾ cup shredded reduced-fat mozzarella cheese (3 ounces)

2 eggs, lightly beaten

¼ cup grated Parmesan cheese

2 teaspoons dried Italian seasoning, crushed

1 14.5-ounce can diced tomatoes with garlic, basil, and oregano, undrained

1 cup bottled roasted red sweet peppers, drained and chopped

1 Preheat oven to 350°F. Cook manicotti shells according to package directions; drain. Rinse with cold water and drain again.

2 Meanwhile, for filling, coat an unheated large nonstick skillet with nonstick cooking spray. Preheat over medium heat. Add mushrooms, carrot, and garlic to hot skillet. Cook for 3 to 5 minutes or just until vegetables are tender, stirring occasionally. Remove from heat; cool slightly. Stir in ricotta cheese, ½ cup of the mozzarella cheese, the eggs, Parmesan cheese, and Italian seasoning. Spoon filling into cooked manicotti shells.

3 For sauce, place tomatoes in a blender or food processor. Cover and blend or process until smooth. Stir in roasted red peppers. Spread about ⅓ cup of the sauce into the bottom of four 12- to 16-ounce ungreased individual baking dishes or a 2-quart rectangular baking dish. Arrange stuffed manicotti shells in individual baking dishes or large baking dish, overlapping shells slightly if necessary. Pour remaining sauce over manicotti.

4 Bake, covered, for 20 to 25 minutes for individual baking dishes, 35 to 40 minutes for large baking dish, or until heated through. Uncover and sprinkle with the remaining ¼ cup mozzarella cheese. Bake for 5 minutes more. Let stand for 10 minutes before serving.

Nutrition facts per serving: 378 cal., 13 g total fat (7 g sat. fat), 141 mg chol., 860 mg sodium, 43 g carb., 3 g dietary fiber, 22 g protein.

double-cheese
MAC AND CHEESE

Prep: 25 minutes
Bake: 25 minutes
Stand: 10 minutes
Oven: 350°F
Makes: 6 servings

12 **ounces penne, bow-tie, or rigatoni pasta**

1 **tablespoon butter**

2 **cloves garlic, minced**

2 **tablespoons all-purpose flour**

2 **cups milk**

2 **cups shredded Port du Salut or Monterey Jack cheese (8 ounces)**

1 **cup shredded American cheese (4 ounces)**

2 **tablespoons snipped fresh oregano, or 1 teaspoon dried oregano, crushed**

½ **cup soft light rye or whole wheat bread crumbs**

 Snipped fresh oregano (optional)

1 Preheat oven to 350°F. Cook pasta according to package directions; drain.

2 Meanwhile, in a large saucepan melt butter over medium heat. Add garlic; cook and stir for 30 seconds. Stir in flour. Gradually stir in milk. Cook and stir until thickened and bubbly. Reduce heat. Gradually add Port du Salut cheese and American cheese, stirring until melted. Remove from heat. Stir in cooked pasta and the 2 tablespoons fresh or dried oregano.

3 Transfer mixture to an ungreased 1½- to 2-quart casserole. Sprinkle with bread crumbs. Bake, uncovered, for about 25 minutes or until heated through. Let stand for 10 minutes before serving. If desired, sprinkle with fresh oregano.

Nutrition facts per serving: 508 cal., 22 g total fat (13 g sat. fat), 80 mg chol., 613 mg sodium, 51 g carb., 2 g dietary fiber, 25 g protein.

linguine WITH GORGONZOLA SAUCE

Start to Finish: 25 minutes
Makes: 4 servings

- 1 **9-ounce package refrigerated whole wheat linguine**
- 1 **pound fresh asparagus, trimmed and cut into 2-inch-long pieces**
- 1 **cup evaporated fat-free milk**
- 2 **ounces reduced-fat cream cheese (Neufchâtel), cubed**
- 2 **ounces Gorgonzola or other blue cheese, crumbled (½ cup)**
- ¼ **teaspoon salt**
- 2 **tablespoons chopped walnuts, toasted**

1 Cook pasta and asparagus together according to package directions for the pasta; drain well. Return pasta and asparagus to pan. Cover and keep warm.

2 Meanwhile, for sauce, in a medium saucepan combine milk, cream cheese, half of the Gorgonzola cheese, and the salt. Bring to boiling over medium heat, whisking constantly; reduce heat. Simmer, uncovered, for 2 minutes, stirring frequently (sauce may appear slightly curdled).

3 Pour sauce over pasta mixture; toss gently to coat. Transfer to shallow bowls. Sprinkle individual servings with remaining Gorgonzola cheese and the walnuts. Serve immediately (sauce will thicken upon standing).

Nutrition facts per serving: 361 cal., 13 g total fat (6 g sat. fat), 42 mg chol., 476 mg sodium, 44 g carb., 7 g dietary fiber, 19 g protein.

spinach AND CHEESE ROLL-UPS

Prep: 30 minutes
Bake: 25 minutes
Oven: 350°F
Makes: 4 servings

⅓ **cup chopped onion (1 small)**

1 **clove garlic, minced**

1 **teaspoon olive oil or cooking oil**

1 **14.5-ounce can diced tomatoes, undrained**

2 **tablespoons tomato paste**

1½ **teaspoons snipped fresh basil, or ½ teaspoon dried basil, crushed**

¼ **teaspoon sugar**
   Pinch of salt and ground black pepper

8 **lasagna noodles**

¾ **cup fat-free or reduced-fat ricotta cheese**

½ **cup shredded part-skim mozzarella cheese (2 ounces)**

2 **tablespoons finely shredded Parmesan cheese**

2 **teaspoons snipped fresh basil, or ½ teaspoon dried basil or Italian seasoning, crushed**

1 **10-ounce package frozen chopped spinach, thawed and well drained**

1 **egg white, lightly beaten**

1 For sauce, in a medium saucepan cook onion and garlic in hot oil over medium heat until onion is tender, stirring occasionally. Carefully stir in tomatoes, tomato paste, basil, sugar, salt, and pepper. Bring to boiling; reduce heat. Simmer, uncovered, for about 5 minutes or until sauce is desired consistency, stirring occasionally.

2 Meanwhile, cook pasta according to package directions; drain. Rinse with cold water; drain again.

3 Preheat oven to 350°F. In a medium bowl, stir together ricotta cheese, mozzarella cheese, Parmesan cheese, and basil. Add spinach and egg white, stirring to combine.

4 To assemble, evenly spread about ¼ cup of the cheese mixture on each noodle. Roll up from one end. Place two rolls, seam sides down, into each of 4 individual casseroles or 1 larger casserole. Top rolls evenly with sauce. Bake, covered, for about 25 minutes or until heated through.

Nutrition facts per serving: 231 cal., 3 g total fat (0 g sat. fat), 10 mg chol., 425 mg sodium, 39 g carb., 2 g dietary fiber, 20 g protein.

ravioli WITH SPINACH PESTO

Start to Finish: 20 minutes
Makes: 4 servings

- **1 9-ounce package refrigerated four-cheese ravioli or tortellini**
- **12 ounces baby pattypan squash, halved, or yellow summer squash, halved lengthwise and sliced ½ inch thick**
- **3½ cups fresh baby spinach**
- **½ cup torn fresh basil**
- **¼ cup bottled Caesar vinaigrette salad dressing**
- **2 tablespoons water**
- **Shredded Parmesan cheese (optional)**

1 Cook ravioli according to package directions, adding squash for the last 2 minutes of cooking; drain.

2 Meanwhile, for pesto, in a blender combine spinach, basil, dressing, and the water. Cover and blend until smooth, stopping to scrape down blender as needed.

3 Toss ravioli mixture with pesto. Sprinkle with Parmesan.

Nutrition facts per serving: 218 cal., 6 g total fat (2 g sat. fat), 27 mg chol., 525 mg sodium, 31 g carbo., 3 g dietary fiber, 11 g protein.

tomato-basil RIGATONI

Prep: 10 minutes
Cook: 14 minutes
Makes: 6 servings

½ cup dry-packed sun-dried
  tomatoes (about
  3 ounces)

1 16-ounce box rigatoni
  pasta

1½ cups milk

¼ cup tomato-basil-
  flavored cream cheese

4 ounces (4 to 6 slices)
  provolone cheese,
  chopped

1 cup shredded part-skim
  mozzarella cheese

2 teaspoons cornstarch
  mixed with 1 tablespoon
  water

½ cup fresh basil leaves,
  cut into thin strips

  Salt and ground black
  pepper

  Shredded Parmesan
  cheese (optional)

1 Heat a large pot of lightly salted water to boiling. Carefully scoop out 1 cup and pour over sun-dried tomatoes in a small heatproof bowl. Let stand 5 minutes.

2 Meanwhile, cook rigatoni according to package directions. Drain.

3 While pasta cooks, heat milk over medium heat until bubbly. Remove from heat and whisk in cream cheese, provolone, and mozzarella until melted (mixture will be a little stringy). Stir in cornstarch-water mixture and return pan to heat. Bring to a simmer, stirring until smooth.

4 Drain and finely chop sun-dried tomatoes. Stir into pasta, along with sauce and basil. Top with a pinch of salt, a little freshly ground black pepper, and Parmesan, if desired.

Nutrition facts per serving: 493 cal., 14 g total fat (8 g sat. fat), 40 mg chol., 637 mg sodium, 67 g carb., 3 g dietary fiber, 23 g protein.

cheesy MULTIGRAIN SPAGHETTI CASSEROLE

Prep: 25 minutes
Cook: 7 to 8 hours (low)
    or 3½ to 4 hours
    (high)
Makes: 6 servings

2½ cups water

1 10.75-ounce can reduced-fat and reduced-sodium condensed cream of mushroom soup

1 14.5-ounce can no-salt-added diced tomatoes

1 cup sliced celery (2 stalks)

1 cup sliced carrots (2 medium)

1 cup chopped onion (1 large)

2 cloves garlic, minced

1½ teaspoons dried Italian seasoning, crushed

¼ teaspoon salt

¼ teaspoon ground black pepper

1 16-ounce package extra-firm tofu, drained if necessary, cubed

8 ounces multigrain spaghetti, broken, cooked according to package directions

½ cup shredded reduced-fat cheddar cheese (2 ounces)

1 In a 3½- or 4-quart slow cooker, whisk together the water and soup. Stir in undrained tomatoes, the celery, carrot, onion, garlic, Italian seasoning, salt, and pepper.

2 Cover and cook on low-heat setting for 7 to 8 hours or high-heat setting for 3½ to 4 hours.

3 Gently stir in tofu cubes and spaghetti. Sprinkle each serving with cheese.

Nutrition facts per serving: 263 cal., 5 g total fat (2 g sat. fat), 7 mg chol., 480 mg sodium, 40 g carb., 5 g dietary fiber, 16 g protein.

tortellini STIR-FRY

Bottled stir-fry sauce provides a dozen seasoning ingredients in a single step. Keep one or two varieties on hand.

Start to Finish: 20 minutes
Makes: 4 servings

1 **9-ounce package refrigerated cheese-filled tortellini**

1 **tablespoon cooking oil**

1 **16-ounce package fresh cut or frozen stir-fry vegetables (such as broccoli, pea pods, carrots, and celery)**

¾ **cup peanut stir-fry sauce**

¼ **cup chopped dry-roasted cashews**

1 Cook tortellini according to package directions. Drain.

2 In a wok or large skillet, heat oil over medium-high heat. Add vegetables; cook and stir for 3 to 5 minutes (7 to 8 minutes for frozen vegetables) or until crisp-tender. Add tortellini and stir-fry sauce; toss gently to coat. Heat through. Sprinkle with cashews; serve immediately.

Nutrition facts per serving: 400 cal., 16 g total fat (3 g sat. fat), 30 mg chol., 1256 mg sodium, 48 g carb., 4 g dietary fiber, 18 g protein.

fettuccine AND VEGETABLES ALFREDO

Start to Finish: 20 minutes
Makes: 4 servings

1   **16-ounce package frozen sugar snap stir-fry vegetable blend (carrot, snap peas, onion, and mushrooms)**

1   **cup frozen sweet soybeans (edamame)**

1   **9-ounce package refrigerated fettuccine**

1   **16-ounce jar Alfredo pasta sauce**

½   **cup finely shredded Parmesan cheese**

¼   **cup milk**

2   **tablespoons purchased basil pesto**

1   In a 4-quart Dutch oven, bring a large amount of water to boiling. Add stir-fry vegetable blend and soybeans. Cook for 3 minutes. Add fettuccine; cook for 3 minutes more or according to package directions. Drain mixture and return to Dutch oven.

2   Meanwhile, for sauce, in a medium saucepan heat pasta sauce, ¼ cup of the Parmesan cheese, milk, and pesto until heated through.

3   Add sauce to pasta mixture; toss to coat. Top with remaining ¼ cup Parmesan cheese.

Nutrition facts per serving: 691 cal., 37 g total fat (16 g sat. fat), 117 mg chol., 1107 mg sodium, 61 g carb., 7 g dietary fiber, 28 g protein.

easy PASTA PRIMAVERA

Substitute elbow macaroni, rotini, or whatever pasta you have on hand for the wagon wheels.

Start to Finish: 25 minutes
Makes: 4 servings

8 ounces wagon wheel pasta

1 16-ounce package desired frozen mixed vegetables

½ of an 8-ounce tub cream cheese spread with chive and onion

¼ to ½ cup milk

Salt and ground black pepper

Finely shredded Parmesan cheese

① In a Dutch oven, cook pasta in a large amount of boiling, lightly salted water for 4 minutes. Add frozen vegetables. Cook for about 5 minutes more or until pasta and vegetables are tender; drain. Return pasta mixture to hot pan.

② Add cream cheese spread to pasta mixture. Cook until heated through, stirring occasionally. Stir in enough of the milk to reach desired consistency. Season to taste with salt and pepper. Sprinkle with Parmesan cheese before serving.

Nutrition facts per serving: 412 cal., 12 g total fat (8 g sat. fat), 32 mg chol., 415 mg sodium, 60 g carb., 6 g dietary fiber, 14 g protein.

soba-vegetable TOSS

Start to Finish: 35 minutes
Makes: 4 servings

6 ounces soba (buckwheat noodles) or multigrain spaghetti

1 tablespoon toasted sesame oil

5 cups broccoli florets

3 medium yellow and/or red sweet peppers, seeded and cut into thin strips

6 medium scallions, bias-sliced into 1-inch-long pieces

¼ cup bottled plum sauce

1 tablespoon rice vinegar

1 tablespoon soy sauce

½ teaspoon crushed red pepper

2 tablespoons sliced almonds, toasted

Sliced scallions (optional)

① Cook soba according to package directions; drain. Return to hot saucepan. Cover and keep warm.

② Meanwhile, pour toasted sesame oil into a wok or very large skillet. Preheat over medium-high heat. Stir-fry broccoli and sweet peppers in hot oil for 3 minutes. Add scallions. Stir-fry for 1 to 2 minutes more or until vegetables are crisp-tender. Add plum sauce, rice vinegar, soy sauce, and crushed red pepper; stir to coat vegetables with sauce. Heat through. Serve immediately with soba. Sprinkle with sliced almonds and, if desired, additional sliced scallions.

Nutrition facts per serving: 313 cal., 6 g total fat (1 g sat. fat), 0 mg chol., 737 mg sodium, 59 g carb., 7 g dietary fiber, 12 g protein.

udon NOODLES WITH TOFU

Look for Japanese udon noodles near the Asian ingredients in your supermarket, or use linguine.

8 **ounces udon noodles or whole wheat linguine**

2 **6- to 8-ounce packages smoked teriyaki-flavored or plain firm tofu, cut into ½-inch pieces**

1½ **cups chopped cucumber**

1 **large carrot, cut into thin bite-size pieces**

½ **cup sliced scallions**
   Ginger-Soy Vinaigrette*

1 Cook pasta according to package directions; drain. Cool pasta slightly.

2 Meanwhile, in a large bowl combine tofu, cucumber, carrot, and scallions. Add drained pasta; toss gently to mix.

3 Drizzle Ginger-Soy Vinaigrette onto cooked pasta mixture. Toss gently to coat.

*Ginger-Soy Vinaigrette: In a small bowl, whisk together 2 tablespoons rice vinegar or cider vinegar, 1 tablespoon toasted sesame oil, 2 teaspoons reduced-sodium soy sauce, 4 minced cloves garlic, 1 teaspoon grated fresh ginger, and ¼ teaspoon crushed red pepper. Makes ¼ cup.

Nutrition facts per serving: 231 cal., 4 g total fat (0 g sat. fat), 0 mg chol., 571 mg sodium, 39 g carb., 3 g dietary fiber, 7 g protein.

Make-Ahead Directions: Prepare as directed. Cover and chill for up to 6 hours.

baked STUFFED SHELLS

To assure a creamy rather than runny filling, be sure to use extra-firm, silken-style tofu and finely shredded Parmesan or Romano cheese.

Prep: 40 minutes
Bake: 37 minutes
Stand: 10 minutes
Oven: 350°F
Makes: 6 servings (2 shells per serving)

1 teaspoon olive oil

½ cup chopped onion

2 cloves garlic, minced

1 14.5-ounce can no-salt-added diced tomatoes, undrained

1 8-ounce can no-salt-added tomato sauce

1 tablespoon snipped fresh basil, or ½ teaspoon dried basil, crushed

2 teaspoons snipped fresh oregano, or ½ teaspoon dried oregano, crushed

¼ teaspoon salt

12 jumbo shell macaroni

1 12.3-ounce package extra-firm, silken-style tofu

¼ cup refrigerated or frozen egg product, thawed, or 1 egg, lightly beaten

½ cup finely shredded Parmesan or Pecorino Romano cheese

¼ teaspoon ground black pepper

½ cup shredded reduced-fat mozzarella cheese (2 ounces)

2 tablespoons shredded fresh basil (optional)

1 Preheat oven to 350°F. For sauce, in a medium saucepan heat oil over medium heat. Add onion and garlic; cook and stir for about 3 minutes or until onion is tender. Carefully add tomatoes, tomato sauce, dried basil and oregano (if using), and salt. Bring to boiling; reduce heat. Simmer, uncovered, for about 15 minutes or until desired consistency. Remove from heat; stir in snipped fresh basil and oregano (if using). Set aside ¾ cup of the sauce; spoon the remaining sauce into a 2-quart rectangular baking dish. Set aside.

2 Meanwhile, cook pasta according to package directions; drain. Rinse with cold water; drain again.

3 For filling, place tofu in a blender or food processor. Cover and blend or process until smooth. Add egg, Parmesan cheese, and pepper; cover and blend or process just until combined. Spoon about 3 tablespoons of the filling into each pasta shell. Arrange filled shells, filling side up, atop sauce in baking dish. Spoon the reserved ¾ cup sauce over top.

4 Bake, covered, for about 35 minutes or until heated through. Uncover and sprinkle with mozzarella cheese. Bake, uncovered, for about 2 minutes more or until cheese is melted. Let stand for 10 minutes before serving. If desired, top with shredded fresh basil.

Nutrition facts per serving: 234 cal., 5 g total fat (2 g sat. fat), 10 mg chol., 357 mg sodium, 32 g carb., 3 g dietary fiber, 14 g protein.

pasta WITH RED PEPPER SAUCE

Sometimes you need a break from ordinary pasta sauce. Sweet red pepper sauce replaces chunky meat sauce and cooks in less time.

Prep: 20 minutes
Bake: 20 minutes
Cool: 20 minutes
Oven: 400°F
Makes: 5 servings

6 **medium red sweet peppers (8 to 10 ounces each)**

4 **cloves garlic, peeled**

10 **ounces pasta (such as mafalda or penne)**

1 **cup water**

1 **6-ounce can tomato paste**

½ **cup loosely packed fresh basil, or 2 teaspoons dried basil, crushed**

2 **tablespoons balsamic vinegar**

¼ **teaspoon salt**

Finely shredded Parmesan cheese (optional)

1 Preheat oven to 400°F. Cut peppers lengthwise into quarters; remove stems, seeds, and membranes. Place, cut side down, on a large foil-lined baking sheet. Add garlic cloves to baking sheet. Bake for about 20 minutes or until peppers are tender and lightly browned. Cool for about 20 minutes or until cool enough to handle.

2 Meanwhile, cook pasta according to package directions; drain and keep warm.

3 Place half each of the sweet peppers, garlic, the water, tomato paste, basil, and vinegar in a blender container or food processor bowl. Cover and blend or process until mixture is nearly smooth. Transfer to a medium saucepan. Repeat with remaining sweet peppers, garlic, water, tomato paste, basil, and vinegar. Stir in salt. Cook and stir sauce over medium-low heat until heated through.

4 To serve, spoon sauce over hot cooked pasta. If desired, sprinkle with Parmesan cheese.

Nutrition facts per serving: 291 cal., 1 g total fat (0 g sat. fat), 0 mg chol., 145 mg sodium, 60 g carb., 5 g dietary fiber, 11 g protein.

vegetables

Zesty Vegetable Enchiladas,
page 214

bumper-crop ZUCCHINI PANCAKES

These golden appetizers or dinnertime treats, flavored with Parmesan cheese and onion, will reign as a favorite pancake recipe. The secret ingredient is zucchini.

Prep: 20 minutes
Stand: 15 minutes
Cook: 4 to 6 minutes
    per batch
Makes: about 30 pancakes

**4 to 5 medium zucchini
(about 1½ pounds)**

¾ teaspoon salt

4 eggs

1 clove garlic, minced

¾ cup all-purpose flour

**½ cup grated Parmesan
cheese**

**1 tablespoon finely
chopped onion**

**¼ teaspoon ground black
pepper**

Sour cream (optional)

1 Trim and coarsely shred zucchini (you should have about 5 cups). In a large bowl, toss zucchini with salt. Place in a colander or sieve. Place a plate or 9-inch pie plate on top of zucchini and weight down with cans or another bowl. Let drain in the sink or over a bowl for 15 minutes. Discard liquid.

2 In the large bowl, beat eggs and garlic. Stir in flour, Parmesan cheese, onion, and pepper until just moistened (batter should be lumpy). Stir in shredded zucchini until just combined (mixture will be thick).

3 For each zucchini pancake, spoon a rounded tablespoon of batter onto a hot, lightly oiled griddle or heavy skillet, spreading to form a 3-inch circle. Cook over medium heat for 2 to 3 minutes on each side or until the pancake is golden brown. (Reduce heat to medium-low if pancakes brown too quickly.) Keep pancakes warm in a low oven while cooking remaining pancakes.

4 Serve warm topped with a dollop of sour cream, if desired. Or cool, and place in layers in a freezer container with waxed paper between layers. To reheat, preheat oven to 425°F. Place frozen pancakes in a single layer on a greased baking sheet. Bake, uncovered, for 8 to 10 minutes or until hot and slightly crisp.

Nutrition facts per pancake: 31 cal., 1 g total fat (0 g sat. fat), 29 mg chol., 90 mg sodium, 3 g carb., 0 g dietary fiber, 2 g protein.

tomato-zucchini TART

Prep: 15 minutes
Bake: 12 minutes
Oven: 400°F/350°F
Makes: 6 servings

1 rolled refrigerated pie
   crust
1 4.4-ounce package light
   herb cheese spread, such
   as Boursin
4 medium ripe tomatoes
   (about 1 pound total),
   thinly sliced, patted dry
2 medium zucchini (about
   1 pound total), sliced
   into ¼-inch coins
⅛ teaspoon salt
⅛ teaspoon ground black
   pepper
   Fresh thyme, for garnish

1 Preheat oven to 400°F. Coat a 9-inch tart pan with nonstick cooking spray.

2 Fit pie crust into tart pan and remove excess dough from around edge. Prick the bottom of the crust all over with a fork. Bake for 12 minutes. Cool. Reduce oven to 350°F.

3 Spread cheese evenly over bottom of crust. Alternately fan tomato and zucchini slices in a decorative fashion. Sprinkle with salt and pepper.

4 Bake for 40 minutes or until nicely browned and zucchini slices are fork-tender. Garnish with fresh thyme; cool slightly and serve.

Nutrition facts per serving: 269 cal., 19 g total fat (10 g sat. fat), 31 mg chol., 318 mg sodium, 24 g carb., 2 g dietary fiber, 4 g protein.

zesty VEGETABLE ENCHILADAS

Prep: 30 minutes
Bake: 15 minutes
Oven: 350°F
Makes: 4 servings

1⅓ cups water

½ cup dried brown lentils, rinsed and drained

8 8-inch flour tortillas

1 cup thinly sliced carrots (2 medium)

2 small zucchini or yellow summer squash, quartered lengthwise and sliced (2 cups)

1 teaspoon ground cumin

1 8-ounce can tomato sauce

1 cup shredded reduced-fat Monterey Jack cheese (4 ounces)

Dash of bottled hot pepper sauce (optional)

1 14.5-ounce can Mexican-style stewed tomatoes, undrained and cut up

Fresh cilantro sprigs (optional)

1 In a medium saucepan, combine the water and lentils. Bring to boiling; reduce heat. Simmer, covered, for 25 to 30 minutes or until lentils are tender; drain.

2 Preheat oven to 350°F. Coat a 2-quart rectangular baking dish with cooking spray; set aside. Stack tortillas and wrap tightly in foil. Bake for about 10 minutes or until warm.

3 Lightly coat an unheated large skillet with cooking spray. Preheat over medium heat. Add carrots. Cook and stir for 2 minutes. Add zucchini and cumin. Cook and stir for 2 to 3 minutes or until vegetables are crisp-tender. Remove from heat. Stir in drained lentils, tomato sauce, ¾ cup of the cheese, and, if desired, hot pepper sauce.

4 Divide lentil mixture among warm tortillas; roll up tortillas. Arrange tortillas, seam sides down, in the prepared baking dish. Sprinkle with the remaining ¼ cup cheese. Spoon tomatoes over tortillas.

5 Bake, uncovered, for 15 to 20 minutes or until heated through. If desired, garnish with cilantro.

Nutrition facts per serving: 450 cal., 15 g total fat (4 g sat. fat), 20 mg chol., 929 mg sodium, 57 g carb., 11 g dietary fiber, 22 g protein.

vegetable CASSEROLE WITH BARLEY AND BULGUR

Prep: 15 minutes
Bake: 1¼ hours
Stand: 5 minutes
Oven: 350°F
Makes: 4 servings

1 **14.5- to 18.5-ounce can ready-to-serve lentil soup**

1 **15-ounce can black beans, rinsed and drained**

2 **medium carrots, sliced (1 cup)**

1 **cup small fresh mushrooms, quartered**

1 **cup frozen whole kernel corn**

½ **cup regular barley**

½ **cup water**

⅓ **cup bulgur**

¼ **cup chopped onion**

½ **teaspoon ground black pepper**

¼ **teaspoon salt**

½ **cup shredded cheddar cheese (2 ounces)**

① Preheat oven to 350°F. In an ungreased 2-quart casserole, combine soup, beans, carrots, mushrooms, corn, barley, water, bulgur, onion, pepper, and salt.

② Bake, covered, for about 1¼ hours or until barley and bulgur are tender, stirring twice. Stir again; sprinkle with cheese. Let stand, covered, for about 5 minutes or until cheese is melted.

Nutrition facts per serving: 384 cal., 8 g total fat (3 g sat. fat), 15 mg chol., 929 mg sodium, 66 g carb., 17 g dietary fiber, 22 g protein.

vegetable CURRY

Indian-style curry is known for its lively flavors. Curry, cumin, garam masala, and cayenne pepper all contribute to this flavorful dish. You'll find garam masala in Indian markets and the gourmet sections of some supermarkets.

Start to Finish: 35 minutes
Makes: 6 servings

- **1 large red onion, halved and cut into thin wedges**
- **1 tablespoon olive oil**
- **2 teaspoons curry powder**
- **1 teaspoon ground cumin**
- **¼ teaspoon garam masala**
- **⅛ teaspoon cayenne pepper**
- **3 cups cauliflower florets**
- **1 14.5-ounce can diced tomatoes, undrained**
- **2 medium potatoes, peeled and cut into 1-inch cubes (about 1½ cups)**
- **2 medium sweet potatoes, peeled and cut into 1-inch cubes (about 1½ cups)**
- **1½ cups vegetable broth or water**
- **¼ teaspoon salt**
- **¼ teaspoon ground black pepper**
- **1 cup loose-pack frozen peas**
- **3 cups hot cooked couscous or brown rice**

1 In a large saucepan, cook onion in hot oil over medium heat for about 5 minutes or until tender. Add curry powder, cumin, garam masala, and cayenne pepper. Cook and stir for 1 minute.

2 Stir in cauliflower, tomatoes, potatoes, sweet potatoes, broth, salt, and black pepper. Bring to boiling; reduce heat. Simmer, covered, for 10 to 12 minutes or until potatoes are tender. Stir in peas; heat through. Serve over couscous or brown rice.

Nutrition facts per serving: 233 cal., 3 g total fat (0 g sat. fat), 0 mg chol., 513 mg sodium, 45 g carb., 6 g dietary fiber, 7 g protein.

tofu AND EGGPLANT

Start to Finish: 30 minutes
Makes: 4 servings

¾ **cup cold water**

3 **tablespoons dry sherry**

2 **tablespoons reduced-sodium soy sauce**

2 **teaspoons cornstarch**

1 **to 2 teaspoons Asian chili sauce**

1 **teaspoon sugar**

1 **tablespoon cooking oil**

2 **Japanese eggplants, halved lengthwise and cut into ¼-inch-thick slices**

2 **medium red sweet peppers, seeded and cut into strips**

1 **tablespoon grated fresh ginger**

2 **to 3 cloves garlic, minced**

12 **to 16 ounces firm tofu, cut into ½-inch cubes**

2 **cups hot cooked brown rice**

Fresh cilantro or basil leaves (optional)

1 For sauce, in a small bowl stir together the water, dry sherry, soy sauce, cornstarch, chili sauce, and sugar.

2 In a large nonstick skillet or wok, heat oil over medium-high heat. Add eggplants and sweet peppers. Cook for 3 to 4 minutes or just until eggplant is tender, stirring often. Remove eggplant mixture from skillet. Add ginger and garlic to skillet; cook for 1 minute. Stir sauce and add to skillet. Cook and stir until thickened and bubbly. Cook and stir for 1 minute more. Add eggplant mixture and tofu to skillet; gently stir to combine. Heat through. Serve over hot cooked rice. If desired, garnish with cilantro or basil leaves.

Nutrition facts per serving: 272 cal., 8 g total fat (1 g sat. fat), 0 mg chol., 334 mg sodium, 38 g carb., 7 g dietary fiber, 11 g protein.

eggplant PARMESAN CASSEROLE

If you love hearty food, put Eggplant Parmesan in your repertoire. It's one of the most robust and filling vegetarian dishes around.

Prep: 30 minutes
Bake: 20 minutes
Stand: 10 minutes
Oven: 350°F
Makes: 6 servings

1 **egg**

½ **cup milk**

¾ **cup all-purpose flour**

¼ **teaspoon salt**

¼ **teaspoon ground black pepper**

1 **large eggplant (1¼ to 1½ pounds), peeled (if desired) and sliced ½ inch thick**

2 **tablespoons cooking oil**

1 **14.5-ounce can diced tomatoes with green pepper and onion**

1 **10.75-ounce can condensed tomato soup**

1 **teaspoon dried Italian seasoning, crushed**

¼ **teaspoon ground black pepper**

1 **cup shredded mozzarella cheese (4 ounces)**

¼ **cup shredded Parmesan cheese**

1 In a shallow dish, whisk together egg and milk. In another shallow dish, combine flour, salt, and ¼ teaspoon pepper. Dip eggplant slices into egg mixture, then into flour mixture, turning to coat both sides. In a large nonstick skillet, cook eggplant slices, a few at a time, in hot oil over medium-high heat for 4 to 6 minutes or until golden, turning once. (If necessary, add additional oil.) Drain eggplant slices on paper towels.

2 Preheat oven to 350°F. In a medium saucepan, combine undrained tomatoes, soup, Italian seasoning, and ¼ teaspoon pepper. Bring to boiling over medium heat, stirring occasionally.

3 Layer half of the eggplant slices in a greased 2-quart rectangular baking dish, cutting slices to fit. Top with half of the tomato mixture; sprinkle with ½ cup of the mozzarella cheese. Repeat layers. Sprinkle with Parmesan cheese.

4 Bake, uncovered, for about 20 minutes or until heated through. Let stand for 10 minutes before serving.

Nutrition facts per serving: 342 cal., 17 g total fat (8 g sat. fat), 68 mg chol., 1110 mg sodium, 31 g carb., 4 g dietary fiber, 18 g protein.

spring PEA RISOTTO

Serve this classic Venetian dish with a simple fresh tomato salad and some Italian bread, and you're set for a lovely Northern Italian dinner.

Start to Finish: 30 minutes
Makes: 4 servings

- 2 **tablespoons olive oil**
- 1 **medium onion, chopped (½ cup)**
- 2 **cloves garlic, minced**
- 1 **cup arborio rice**
- 2 **14-ounce cans vegetable broth**
- 1 **cup frozen tiny or regular-size shelled peas**
- ¼ **cup coarsely shredded carrot**
- 2 **cups fresh spinach, shredded**
- ¼ **cup grated Parmesan cheese**
- 1 **tablespoon snipped fresh thyme**

1 In a large saucepan, heat oil over medium heat. Cook onion and garlic until onion is tender. Add the uncooked rice. Cook and stir about 5 minutes or until rice is golden.

2 Meanwhile, in a medium saucepan, bring broth to boiling; reduce heat and simmer. Carefully add 1 cup of the broth to the rice mixture, stirring constantly. Continue to cook and stir over medium heat until liquid is absorbed.

3 Add another 1 cup of the broth to the rice mixture, stirring constantly. Continue to cook and stir until liquid is absorbed. Add another 1 cup broth, ½ cup at a time, stirring constantly until the broth has been absorbed. (This should take 18 to 20 minutes.)

4 Stir in remaining ½ cup broth, the peas, and carrot. Cook and stir until the rice is slightly creamy and just tender.

5 Stir in the spinach, Parmesan cheese, and thyme; heat through. Serve immediately.

Nutrition facts per serving: 263 cal., 10 g total fat (2 g sat. fat), 5 mg chol., 1047 mg sodium, 388 g carb., 3 g dietary fiber, 9 g protein.

spinach AND
FETA CASSEROLE

Prep: 20 minutes
Bake: 45 minutes
Oven: 350°F
Makes: 4 servings

3 eggs, lightly beaten

2 cups cream-style cottage cheese

1 10-ounce package frozen chopped spinach, thawed and well drained

⅓ cup crumbled feta cheese

¼ cup butter, melted

3 tablespoons all-purpose flour

2 teaspoons dried minced onion

Pinch of ground nutmeg

1 Preheat oven to 350°F. Grease a 1½-quart casserole. In a large bowl, combine eggs, cottage cheese, spinach, feta cheese, melted butter, flour, dried onion, and nutmeg. Transfer mixture to the prepared casserole.

2 Bake, uncovered, for about 45 minutes or until center is nearly set (160°F).

Nutrition facts per serving: 172 cal., 12 g total fat (7 g sat. fat), 109 mg chol., 392 mg sodium, 6 g carb., 2 g dietary fiber, 11 g protein.

223

223

mushroom-vegetable
FAJITAS

Prep: 25 minutes
Grill: 20 minutes
Makes: 4 servings

1 small avocado, halved, pitted, and peeled

1 tablespoon lime juice

1 clove garlic, minced

½ teaspoon ground cumin

½ teaspoon dried oregano, crushed

¼ teaspoon salt

⅛ teaspoon ground black pepper

3 small fresh portobello mushrooms, stems and gills removed

2 medium red, yellow and/or green sweet peppers, halved, stemmed, and seeded

½ of a medium red onion, cut into ½-inch-thick slices

Nonstick cooking spray

4 7- to 8-inch whole wheat flour tortillas

Lime wedges (optional)

1. Place the avocado halves in a small bowl. With a potato masher or fork, mash avocado until nearly smooth. Stir in lime juice and garlic. Cover the surface of the avocado mixture with plastic wrap and chill until ready to serve.

2. In a small bowl, combine cumin, oregano, salt, and black pepper. Coat mushrooms, sweet pepper halves, and red onion slices with nonstick cooking spray. Sprinkle cumin mixture on vegetables.

3. For a charcoal grill, place mushrooms, sweet pepper halves, and onion slices on rack of an uncovered grill directly over medium coals. Grill until vegetables are crisp-tender, turning once halfway through grilling and removing vegetables when they are done. Allow 8 to 10 minutes for the sweet peppers, 10 to 15 minutes for the mushrooms, and 15 to 20 minutes for the onion slices. (For a gas grill, preheat grill. Reduce heat to medium. Place vegetables on grill rack directly over heat. Cover and grill as above.)

4. Place tortillas on grill rack directly over medium coals. Grill for 20 to 30 seconds or until warm, turning once. Remove from grill and cover to keep warm. Thinly slice mushrooms and sweet peppers. Coarsely chop onion slices.

5. Spread avocado mixture on the warm tortillas. Divide vegetables among the tortillas. Fold over. If desired, serve with lime wedges.

Nutrition facts per serving: 233 cal., 10 g total fat (2 g sat. fat), 0 mg chol., 475 mg sodium, 26 g carb., 15 g dietary fiber, 11 g protein.

polenta WITH MUSHROOM SAUCE AND CHEESE

Prep: 15 minutes
Bake: 25 minutes
Oven: 350°F
Makes: 6 servings

3 cups sliced fresh mushrooms (8 ounces)

1 15-ounce container refrigerated marinara sauce

1 16-ounce tube refrigerated cooked plain polenta

¼ cup thinly sliced fresh basil

1 cup shredded Italian 4-cheese blend (4 ounces)

1 Preheat oven to 350°F. Coat a large skillet with cooking spray. Heat over medium heat. Add mushrooms to skillet; cook over medium heat for 5 to 7 minutes or until tender, stirring occasionally. Remove from heat and stir in marinara sauce.

2 Cut polenta into ½-inch slices. Arrange in the bottom of a greased 2-quart square baking dish. Top with basil. Sprinkle ½ cup of the cheese over basil. Top with the sauce. Bake, uncovered, for 20 minutes or until heated through. Sprinkle with the remaining ½ cup cheese. Return to oven and bake for 5 minutes more or until cheese is melted.

Nutrition facts per serving: 186 cal., 8 g total fat (3 g sat. fat), 13 mg chol., 684 mg sodium, 20 g carb., 4 g dietary fiber, 9 g protein.

savory STUFFED PORTOBELLOS

Portobello mushrooms have a rich flavor and dense, meaty texture. The stems tend to be woody, so trim and discard them.

Prep: 35 minutes
Bake: 15 minutes
Oven: 350°F
Makes: 6 servings

½ cup chopped onion
(1 medium)

4 cloves garlic, minced,
or 2 teaspoons bottled
minced garlic

1 6.75- to 8-ounce package
rice pilaf with lentils mix

1 6-ounce jar marinated
artichoke hearts

6 medium portobello
mushroom caps (about
4 inches in diameter)

¼ cup finely shredded
Parmesan cheese
(optional)

1 Preheat oven to 350°F. Coat a medium saucepan with cooking spray. Preheat over medium-high heat. Add onion and garlic; cook until tender. In the same saucepan with the onion and garlic, cook rice pilaf mix according to package directions.

2 Meanwhile, drain artichoke hearts, reserving marinade. Coarsely chop artichokes. Cut off mushroom stems even with caps; discard stems. If desired, remove gills from undersides of caps. Brush mushrooms with some of the reserved marinade; discard any remaining marinade. Place mushroom caps, stemmed side up, in an ungreased shallow baking pan.

3 Bake, uncovered, for 15 to 20 minutes or until mushrooms are tender. Transfer to individual plates, stemmed side up. Stir artichoke hearts and, if desired, cheese into hot pilaf mixture; spoon into baked mushroom caps.

Nutrition facts per serving: 288 cal., 14 g total fat (5 g sat. fat), 16 mg chol., 817 mg sodium, 31 g carb., 4 g dietary fiber, 20 g protein.

peppers STUFFED WITH CRANBERRY BULGUR

Start to Finish: 30 minutes
Makes: 4 servings

1 **14-ounce can vegetable broth**

½ **cup shredded carrot (1 medium)**

¼ **cup chopped onion**

¾ **cup bulgur**

⅓ **cup dried cranberries, cherries, or raisins**

2 **large or 4 small green, red, or yellow sweet peppers**

¾ **cup shredded Muenster, brick, or mozzarella cheese (3 ounces)**

½ **cup water**

2 **tablespoons sliced almonds or chopped pecans, toasted**

1 In a large skillet, combine the broth, carrot, and onion. Bring to boiling; reduce heat. Simmer, covered, for 5 minutes. Stir in bulgur and cranberries. Remove from heat. Cover and let stand for 5 minutes. Drain off excess liquid, if necessary.

2 Meanwhile, halve the sweet peppers lengthwise, removing the seeds and membranes. Stir shredded cheese into bulgur mixture; spoon into sweet pepper halves.

3 Place sweet pepper halves in skillet; add the water. Bring to boiling; reduce heat. Simmer, covered, for 5 to 10 minutes or until sweet peppers are crisp-tender and bulgur mixture is heated through. Sprinkle with nuts.

Nutrition facts per serving: 260 cal., 9 g total fat (4 g sat. fat), 20 mg chol., 552 mg sodium, 37 g carb., 8 g dietary fiber, 10 g protein.

spaghetti SQUASH WITH CHUNKY TOMATO SAUCE

Prep: 25 minutes
Cook: 15 minutes
Makes: 4 servings

1 tablespoon olive oil

1 cup coarsely chopped zucchini

⅔ cup chopped onion

½ cup shredded carrot

2 cloves garlic, minced

1 14.5-ounce can diced tomatoes, undrained

1 8-ounce can tomato sauce

2 tablespoons tomato paste

2 teaspoons dried Italian seasoning, crushed

⅛ teaspoon ground black pepper

4 cups cooked spaghetti squash*

¼ cup shredded Parmesan cheese

Small fresh basil leaves (optional)

1 For chunky tomato sauce, in a large saucepan heat oil over medium heat. Add zucchini, onion, carrot, and garlic; cook until tender, stirring occasionally. Add diced tomatoes, tomato sauce, tomato paste, Italian seasoning, and pepper. Bring to boiling; reduce heat. Simmer, uncovered, for 15 minutes, stirring occasionally.

2 Serve chunky tomato sauce over spaghetti squash. Sprinkle with Parmesan cheese. If desired, garnish with basil leaves.

Nutrition facts per serving: 154 cal., 6 g total fat (1 g sat. fat), 4 mg chol., 610 mg sodium, 23 g carb., 3 g dietary fiber, 5 g protein.

*Tip: To cook spaghetti squash, cut a 3-pound spaghetti squash in half lengthwise; remove seeds and strings. Place one half, cut side down, in a microwave-safe baking dish. Using a fork, prick the skin all over. Microwave on 100% power (high) for 6 to 7 minutes or until tender when pierced with a fork; carefully remove from baking dish. Repeat with the other half. (Or preheat oven to 350°F. Place both halves, cut sides down, in a shallow baking pan and bake for 30 to 40 minutes or until tender.) Cool slightly; using two forks, shred and separate the squash pulp into strands. Makes about 4 cups.

sweet AND SOUR CABBAGE ROLLS

Raisins and brown sugar sweeten purchased marinara sauce while a splash of lemon juice adds a pleasing tartness. The resulting tangy-sweet sauce complements these bean-and-rice-filled cabbage rolls.

Prep: 1 hour
Cook: 7 to 9 hours (low)
       or 3½ to 4½ hours
       (high)
Makes: 4 servings

- 1 **large head green cabbage**
- 1 **15-ounce can black beans or red kidney beans, rinsed and drained**
- 1 **cup cooked brown rice**
- ½ **cup chopped carrots**
- ½ **cup chopped celery**
- 1 **medium onion, chopped**
- 1 **clove garlic, minced**
- 3½ **cups marinara sauce or meatless spaghetti sauce**
- ⅓ **cup raisins**
- 3 **tablespoons lemon juice**
- 1 **tablespoon brown sugar**

1 Remove 8 large outer leaves from head of cabbage. In a Dutch oven, cook cabbage leaves in boiling water for 4 to 5 minutes or just until leaves are limp. Drain cabbage leaves. Trim the thick rib in center of each leaf. Shred 4 cups of the remaining cabbage; place shredded cabbage in a 3½- to 6-quart slow cooker.

2 In a medium bowl, combine beans, rice, carrots, celery, onion, garlic, and ½ cup of the marinara sauce. Divide bean mixture evenly among the 8 cabbage leaves, using about ⅓ cup per leaf. Fold sides of each leaf over filling and roll up.

3 Combine remaining marinara sauce, raisins, lemon juice, and brown sugar. Pour about half of the sauce mixture over shredded cabbage in cooker. Stir to mix. Place cabbage rolls atop shredded cabbage. Top with remaining sauce.

4 Cover and cook on low-heat setting for 7 to 9 hours or on high-heat setting for 3½ to 4½ hours. Carefully remove the cooked cabbage rolls and serve with the shredded cabbage.

Nutrition facts per serving: 406 cal., 12 g total fat (3 g sat. fat), 0 mg chol., 1476 mg sodium, 69 g carb., 15 g dietary fiber, 14 g protein.

scalloped POTATOES AND BEANS

Red kidney and black beans elevate scalloped potatoes from a supporting role to the main attraction. To cut down on prep time, leave the peels on the potatoes.

Prep: 15 minutes
Cook: 8 to 10 hours (low)
or 4 to 5 hours (high)
Makes: 5 servings

- 1 15- to 16-ounce can red kidney beans, rinsed and drained
- 1 15-ounce can black beans, rinsed and drained
- 1 large onion, chopped (1 cup)
- 2 stalks celery, sliced ¼ inch thick (1 cup)
- 1 large green sweet pepper, seeded and chopped (1 cup)
- 1 10.75-ounce can reduced-fat and reduced-sodium condensed cream of mushroom soup
- 4 cloves garlic, minced
- 1 teaspoon dried thyme, crushed
- ¼ teaspoon ground black pepper
- 1 pound potatoes, sliced ¼ inch thick
- 1 cup frozen peas
- 1 cup shredded cheddar cheese (4 ounces; optional)

1. In a large bowl, combine kidney beans, black beans, onion, celery, sweet pepper, soup, garlic, thyme, and black pepper.

2. Spoon half of the bean mixture into a 3½- or 4-quart slow cooker. Top with potatoes, peas, and the remaining bean mixture.

3. Cover and cook on low-heat setting for 8 to 10 hours or on high-heat setting for 4 to 5 hours. If desired, top servings with cheddar cheese.

Nutrition facts per serving: 272 cal., 2 g total fat (0 g sat. fat), 2 mg chol., 656 mg sodium, 55 g carb., 13 g dietary fiber, 16 g protein.

metric information

The charts on this page provide a guide for converting measurements from the U.S. customary system, which is used throughout this book, to the metric system.

PRODUCT DIFFERENCES

Most of the ingredients called for in the recipes in this book are available in most countries. However, some are known by different names. Here are some common American ingredients and their possible counterparts:

- Sugar (white) is granulated, fine granulated, or castor sugar.
- Powdered sugar is icing sugar.
- All-purpose flour is enriched, bleached, or unbleached white household flour. When self-rising flour is used in place of all-purpose flour in a recipe that calls for leavening, omit the leavening agent (baking soda or baking powder) and salt.
- Light-colored corn syrup is golden syrup.
- Cornstarch is cornflour.
- Baking soda is bicarbonate of soda.
- Vanilla or vanilla extract is vanilla essence.
- Green, red, or yellow sweet peppers are capsicums or bell peppers.
- Golden raisins are sultanas.

VOLUME AND WEIGHT

The United States traditionally uses cup measures for liquid and solid ingredients. The chart, top right, shows the approximate imperial and metric equivalents. If you are accustomed to weighing solid ingredients, the following approximate equivalents will be helpful.

- 1 cup butter, castor sugar, or rice = 8 ounces = $1/2$ pound = 250 grams
- 1 cup flour = 4 ounces = $1/4$ pound = 125 grams
- 1 cup icing sugar = 5 ounces = 150 grams

Canadian and U.S. volume for a cup measure is 8 fluid ounces (237 ml), but the standard metric equivalent is 250 ml.

1 British imperial cup is 10 fluid ounces.

In Australia, 1 tablespoon equals 20 ml, and there are 4 teaspoons in the Australian tablespoon.

Spoon measures are used for smaller amounts of ingredients. Although the size of the tablespoon varies slightly in different countries, for practical purposes and for recipes in this book, a straight substitution is all that's necessary. Measurements made using cups or spoons always should be level unless stated otherwise.

COMMON WEIGHT RANGE REPLACEMENTS

Imperial / U.S.	Metric
$1/2$ ounce	15 g
1 ounce	25 g or 30 g
4 ounces ($1/4$ pound)	115 g or 125 g
8 ounces ($1/2$ pound)	225 g or 250 g
16 ounces (1 pound)	450 g or 500 g
$1 1/4$ pounds	625 g
$1 1/2$ pounds	750 g
2 pounds or $2 1/4$ pounds	1,000 g or 1 Kg

OVEN TEMPERATURE EQUIVALENTS

Fahrenheit Setting	Celsius Setting*	Gas Setting
300°F	150°C	Gas Mark 2 (very low)
325°F	160°C	Gas Mark 3 (low)
350°F	180°C	Gas Mark 4 (moderate)
375°F	190°C	Gas Mark 5 (moderate)
400°F	200°C	Gas Mark 6 (hot)
425°F	220°C	Gas Mark 7 (hot)
450°F	230°C	Gas Mark 8 (very hot)
475°F	240°C	Gas Mark 9 (very hot)
500°F	260°C	Gas Mark 10 (extremely hot)
Broil	Broil	Grill

*Electric and gas ovens may be calibrated using Celsius. However, for an electric oven, increase Celsius setting 10 to 20 degrees when cooking above 160°C. For convection or forced air ovens (gas or electric), lower the temperature setting 25°F/10°C when cooking at all heat levels.

BAKING PAN SIZES

Imperial / U.S.	Metric
9×1$1/2$-inch round cake pan	22- or 23×4-cm (1.5 L)
9×1$1/2$-inch pie plate	22- or 23×4-cm (1 L)
8×8×2-inch square cake pan	20×5-cm (2 L)
9×9×2-inch square cake pan	22- or 23×4.5-cm (2.5 L)
11×7×1$1/2$-inch baking pan	28×17×4-cm (2 L)
2-quart rectangular baking pan	30×19×4.5-cm (3 L)
13×9×2-inch baking pan	34×22×4.5-cm (3.5 L)
15×10×1-inch jelly roll pan	40×25×2-cm
9×5×3-inch loaf pan	23×13×8-cm (2 L)
2-quart casserole	2 L

U.S. / STANDARD METRIC EQUIVALENTS

$1/8$ teaspoon = 0.5 ml	$1/3$ cup = 3 fluid ounces = 75 ml
$1/4$ teaspoon = 1 ml	$1/2$ cup = 4 fluid ounces = 125 ml
$1/2$ teaspoon = 2 ml	$1/3$ cup = 5 fluid ounces = 150 ml
1 teaspoon = 5 ml	$3/4$ cup = 6 fluid ounces = 175 ml
1 tablespoon = 15 ml	1 cup = 8 fluid ounces = 250 ml
2 tablespoons = 25 ml	2 cups = 1 pint = 500 ml
$1/4$ cup = 2 fluid ounces = 50 ml	1 quart = 1 liter

index

Note: Page references in *italics* indicate photographs.

A

Appetizers. *See also* **Dips and spreads**
Artichoke-Stuffed New Potatoes, 14
Avocado Pesto–Stuffed Tomatoes, 8
Endive-Mango Appetizers, 16, *17*
Four-Cheese Stuffed Mushrooms, 30
Herbed Deviled Egg Bruschetta, 24
Hummus-and-Cucumber
Bruschetta, 22, *23*
Onion and Olive Focaccia, 25
Spicy Tofu Triangles, 26, *27*
Swiss and Olive Galette, 20, *21*
Triple-Pepper Nachos, 28, *29*
Apricot Iced Tea, *32*, *33*
Apricot-Spinach Salad, 70, *71*
Artichokes
Artichoke and Basil Hero, 104, *105*
Artichoke-Basil Lasagna, *181*, 183
Artichoke-Stuffed New Potatoes, 14
Fontina Cheese and Artichoke
Pizza, 126, *127*
Peppery Artichoke Pitas, 106, *107*
Savory Stuffed Portobellos, 227
Asian Tofu Salad, 82, *83*
A to Z Vegetable Soup, 38, *39*
Avocado Pesto–Stuffed Tomatoes, 8

B

Baked Breakfast Portobellos, 151
Baked Eggs with Cheese and Basil
Sauce, 149
Baked Stuffed Shells, 206
Barley
Beans, Barley, and Tomatoes, 161
Multigrain Pilaf, 178
Risotto-Style Barley and
Vegetables, 179
Vegetable Casserole with Barley and
Bulgur, 215
Vegetable Two-Grain
Casserole, 176, *177*
Beans. *See also* **Black beans;**
Edamame; Lentils; White beans
Bean Burgers, 118, *119*
Bean Burritos, 162, *163*
Chili Bean–Stuffed Peppers, 158, *159*
Greek Garbanzo Salad, 90, *91*
Harvest Chili, 55
Italian Three-Bean and Rice Skillet, 167
Pumpkin, Chickpea, and Red Lentil
Stew, 64
Red Beans Creole, 166
Risotto with Beans and
Vegetables, *153*, 172
Scalloped Potatoes and Beans, 233
Tarragon Bean Salad, 89
Tex-Mex Beans with Cornmeal
Dumplings, 164, *165*
Vegetable Chili with Cheese
Topping, 54
Black beans
Black Bean and Brown Rice Stew, 65
Black Bean Cakes with Salsa, 156, *157*
Black Bean Lasagna, 182
Black Bean Slaw with Soy-Ginger
Dressing, 92, *93*
Poached Eggs with Polenta and
Black Beans, 143
Polenta and Black Beans, 154
Salsa, Bean, and Cheese
Pizza, 128, *129*
Salsa, Black Bean, and Rice Salad, 94
Southwestern Bean and Cheese
Bake, 132, *133*
Spicy Black Beans and Rice, 155

Sweet and Sour Cabbage Rolls, 232
Vegetarian Gumbo, 56, *57*
Blue Cheese and Bean Salad, 95
Breads. *See also* **Tortillas**
Onion and Olive Focaccia, 25
Three-Bread Salad, 75
Broccoli
Deli-Style Pasta Salad, 81
Soba-Vegetable Toss, 202, *203*
Brown Rice Primavera, 173
Brown Rice–Spinach Custards, 174, *175*
Bulgur
Peppers Stuffed with Cranberry
Bulgur, 228, *229*
Tabbouleh with Edamame and Feta,
86, *87*
Thai Bulgur Salad, 84, *85*
Vegetable Casserole with Barley and
Bulgur, 215
Vegetable Two-Grain
Casserole, 176, *177*
Bumper-Crop Zucchini Pancakes, 210, *211*
Burgers
Bean Burgers, 118, *119*
Garden Veggie Burgers, 115
Zucchini-Carrot Burgers, 116, *117*
Butternut Squash Soup with Ravioli, 46, *47*

C

Cabbage
Black Bean Slaw with Soy-Ginger
Dressing, 92, *93*
Sweet and Sour Cabbage Rolls, 232
Caramelized Onion–Blue Cheese
Dip, 18, *19*
Caramelized Onion Soup, *37*, 43
Carrots
Curried Carrot Spread, 15
Roasted Vegetable Dip, 10, *11*
Zucchini-Carrot Burgers, 116, *117*
Cauliflower
Cheesy Potato and Cauliflower
Chowder, 60, *61*
Harvest Chili, 55
Vegetable Curry, 216, *217*

Cheese

Baked Eggs with Cheese and Basil
Sauce, 149

Blue Cheese and Bean Salad, 95

Caramelized Onion–Blue Cheese
Dip, 18, *19*

Cheese and Mushroom Egg
Casserole, 142

Cheese Calzones, 134, *135*

Cheese Manicotti with Roasted
Pepper Sauce, 184, *185*

Cheesy Mexican-Style Vegetable
Soup, 42

Cheesy Multigrain Spaghetti
Casserole, 196, *197*

Cheesy Potato and Cauliflower
Chowder, 60, *61*

Double-Cheese Mac and
Cheese, 186, *187*

Easy Cheesy Quesadillas with
Avocado, Spinach, and Pepper, 130

Eggplant Parmesan Casserole, 220

Fontina and Melon Salad, 69

Fontina Cheese and Artichoke
Pizza, 126, *127*

Four-Cheese Stuffed Mushrooms, 30

Grilled Veggie-Cheese
Sandwiches, 98, *99*

Italian Veggie Burger Bites, 120

Kale–Goat Cheese Frittata, 138

Linguine with Gorgonzola
Sauce, 188

Mock Cheese Soufflé, 137

Pepper Stromzoni, 103

Salsa, Bean, and Cheese
Pizza, 128, *129*

Skillet Vegetables on Cheese
Toast, 136

Southwestern Bean and Cheese
Bake, 132, *133*

Spinach and Cheese Roll-Ups, 189

Spinach and Feta Casserole, 222, *223*

Swiss and Olive Galette, 20, *21*

Walnut-Cheese Risotto, 131

White Bean and Goat Cheese
Wraps, 122

Chili

Harvest Chili, 55

Vegetable Chili with Cheese
Topping, 54

White Bean and Cumin Chili, 52, *53*

Chili Bean–Stuffed Peppers, 158, *159*

Corn Chowder, Jalapeño, 62

Cranberry-Pineapple Cooler, 34, *35*

Cucumbers

Grilled Veggie-Cheese
Sandwiches, 98, *99*

Hummus-and-Cucumber
Bruschetta, 22, *23*

Curried Carrot Spread, 15

Curry, Vegetable, 216, *217*

D

Deli-Style Pasta Salad, 81

Dips and spreads

Caramelized Onion–Blue Cheese
Dip, 18, *19*

Curried Carrot Spread, 15

Edamame-Lemongrass
Hummus, 12, *13*

Eggplant-Garlic Spread, 9

Roasted Vegetable Dip, 10, *11*

Double-Cheese Mac and
Cheese, 186, *187*

Drinks

Apricot Iced Tea, 32, *33*

Cranberry-Pineapple Cooler, 34, *35*

Tofruity Sipper, 31

E

Easy Cheesy Quesadillas with Avocado,
Spinach, and Pepper, 130

Easy Pasta Primavera, 201

Edamame

Beans, Barley, and Tomatoes, 161

Edamame-Lemongrass
Hummus, 12, *13*

Meatless Shepherd's Pie, 160

Multigrain Pilaf, 178

Tabbouleh with Edamame and
Feta, 86, *87*

Thai Bulgur Salad, 84, *85*

Eggplant

Brown Rice Primavera, 173

Eggplant-Garlic Spread, 9

Eggplant Panini, 110, *111*

Eggplant Parmesan Casserole, 220

Grilled Vegetables on Focaccia, 114

Open-Face Ratatouille
Sandwich, 100, *101*

Provençal Vegetable Stew, 63

Tofu and Eggplant, 218, *219*

Eggs

Baked Breakfast Portobellos, 151

Baked Eggs with Cheese and Basil
Sauce, 149

Cheese and Mushroom Egg
Casserole, 142

Egg Salad–Stuffed Tomatoes, 72, *73*

Egg and Vegetable Salad Wraps, 123

Grilled Egg Sandwich, 150

Herbed Deviled Egg Bruschetta, 24

Kale–Goat Cheese Frittata, 138

Mediterranean Frittata, 140, *141*

Oven Omelets with Pesto, *125,* 148

Poached Eggs with Grainy Mustard
Vinaigrette, 144, *145*

Poached Eggs with Polenta and
Black Beans, 143

Spring Crustless Quiche, 146, *147*

Endive-Mango Appetizers, 16, *17*

F

Fettuccine and Vegetables Alfredo, 200

Fontina and Melon Salad, 69

Fontina Cheese and Artichoke
Pizza, 126, *127*

Four-Cheese Stuffed Mushrooms, 30

Fried Rice, 168, *169*

Fruit. *See specific fruits*

G

Garden Veggie Burgers, 115

Ginger Tofu Salad Wraps, 121

Grains. *See* Barley; Bulgur; Polenta; Rice;
Wheat berries

Greek Garbanzo Salad, 90, *91*

Greek Minestrone with Feta, 50, *51*

Greens. *See also* **Spinach**
    Kale–Goat Cheese Frittata, 138
    Layered Southwestern Salad with
        Tortilla Strips, 76, *77*
    Mesclun Salad with Roasted Pears
        and Walnuts, *67*, 68
    Roasted Vegetables over Salad
        Greens, 74
    Three-Bread Salad, 75
Grilled Egg Sandwich, 150
Grilled Vegetables on Focaccia, 114
Grilled Veggie-Cheese Sandwiches, 98, *99*

H

Harvest Chili, 55
Herbed Deviled Egg Bruschetta, 24
Hummus-and-Cucumber
        Bruschetta, 22, *23*

I

Italian Three-Bean and Rice Skillet, 167
Italian Veggie Burger Bites, 120

J

Jalapeño Corn Chowder, 62

K

Kale–Goat Cheese Frittata, 138

L

Layered Southwestern Salad with Tortilla
        Strips, 76, *77*
Lentils
    Lentil- and Rice-Stuffed
        Peppers, 170, *171*
    Pumpkin, Chickpea, and Red Lentil
        Stew, 64
    Zesty Vegetable Enchiladas, *209*, 214
Linguine with Gorgonzola Sauce, 188

M

Mangoes
    Endive-Mango Appetizers, 16, *17*
    Tofruity Sipper, 31
    Tofu Pitas with Mango Salsa, 108
Marinara Sauce with Pasta, 195

Meatless Shepherd's Pie, 160
Mediterranean Frittata, 140, *141*
Melon and Fontina Salad, 69
Mesclun Salad with Roasted Pears and
        Walnuts, *67*, 68
Mexican Fiesta Salad, 78, *79*
Mock Cheese Soufflé, 137
Multigrain Pilaf, 178
Mushrooms
    Baked Breakfast Portobellos, 151
    Cheese and Mushroom Egg
        Casserole, 142
    Four-Cheese Stuffed Mushrooms, 30
    Greek Minestrone with Feta, 50, *51*
    Mushroom, Noodle, and Tofu
        Soup, 48
    Mushroom-Vegetable Fajitas, 224, *225*
    Polenta with Mushroom Sauce and
        Cheese, 226
    Savory Stuffed Portobellos, 227
    Spinach-Mushroom
        Quesadillas, 112, *113*
    Spring Crustless Quiche, 146, *147*
    Tortellini-Vegetable Salad, 80

O

Olives
    Onion and Olive Focaccia, 25
    Swiss and Olive Galette, 20, *21*
Onions
    Caramelized Onion–Blue Cheese
        Dip, 18, *19*
    Caramelized Onion Soup, *37*, 43
    Onion and Olive Focaccia, 25
    Sautéed Onion and Tomato
        Sandwiches, 102
Open-Face Ratatouille Sandwich, 100, *101*
Oven Omelets with Pesto, *125*, 148
Oven-Roasted Vegetable Penne, 194

P

Pasta and noodles
    Artichoke-Basil Lasagna, *181*, 183
    Baked Stuffed Shells, 206
    Black Bean Lasagna, 182

    Butternut Squash Soup with
        Ravioli, 46, *47*
    Cheese Manicotti with Roasted
        Pepper Sauce, 184, *185*
    Cheesy Multigrain Spaghetti
        Casserole, 196, *197*
    Deli-Style Pasta Salad, 81
    Double-Cheese Mac and
        Cheese, 186, *187*
    Easy Pasta Primavera, 201
    Fettuccine and Vegetables
        Alfredo, 200
    Fontina and Melon Salad, 69
    Linguine with Gorgonzola
        Sauce, 188
    Marinara Sauce with Pasta, 195
    Mexican Fiesta Salad, 78, *79*
    Mushroom, Noodle, and Tofu
        Soup, 48
    Oven-Roasted Vegetable Penne, 194
    Pasta with Red Pepper Sauce, 207
    Ravioli with Spinach Pesto, 190, *191*
    Soba-Vegetable Toss, 202, *203*
    Spinach and Cheese Roll-Ups, 189
    Tomato-Basil Rigatoni, 192, *193*
    Tortellini Stir-Fry, 198, *199*
    Tortellini-Vegetable Salad, 80
    Udon Noodles with Tofu, 204, *205*
Pears, Roasted, and Walnuts, Mesclun
        Salad with, *67*, 68
Peas, Spring, Risotto, 221
Peppers
    Brown Rice Primavera, 173
    Chili Bean–Stuffed Peppers, 158, *159*
    Grilled Vegetables on Focaccia, 114
    Jalapeño Corn Chowder, 62
    Lentil- and Rice-Stuffed
        Peppers, 170, *171*
    Pasta with Red Pepper Sauce, 207
    Peppers Stuffed with Cranberry
        Bulgur, 228, *229*
    Pepper Stromzoni, 103
    Roasted Vegetable Dip, 10, *11*
    Soba-Vegetable Toss, 202, *203*
    Triple-Pepper Nachos, 28, *29*

Peppery Artichoke Pitas, 106, *107*
Pizza
Fontina Cheese and Artichoke
Pizza, 126, *127*
Salsa, Bean, and Cheese
Pizza, 128, *129*
Poached Eggs with Grainy Mustard
Vinaigrette, 144, *145*
Poached Eggs with Polenta and Black
Beans, 143
Polenta
Poached Eggs with Polenta and
Black Beans, 143
Polenta and Black Beans, 154
Polenta with Mushroom Sauce and
Cheese, 226
Potatoes
Artichoke-Stuffed New Potatoes, 14
Bean and Potato Chowder, 58, *59*
Cheesy Potato and Cauliflower
Chowder, 60, *61*
Meatless Shepherd's Pie, 160
Roasted Garlic Potato Soup, 44, *45*
Scalloped Potatoes and Beans, 233
Provençal Vegetable Stew, 63
Pumpkin, Chickpea, and Red Lentil
Stew, 64

R
Ravioli with Spinach Pesto, 190, *191*
Red Beans Creole, 166
Rice. *See also* **Risotto**
Black Bean and Brown Rice Stew, 65
Brown Rice Primavera, 173
Brown Rice–Spinach
Custards, 174, *175*
Fried Rice, 168, *169*
Italian Three-Bean and Rice
Skillet, 167
Lentil- and Rice-Stuffed
Peppers, 170, *171*
Multigrain Pilaf, 178
Red Beans Creole, 166
Salsa, Black Bean, and Rice Salad, 94
Savory Stuffed Portobellos, 227
Spicy Black Beans and Rice, 155

Risotto
Risotto with Beans and
Vegetables, *153*, 172
Spring Pea Risotto, 221
Walnut-Cheese Risotto, 131
Risotto-Style Barley and Vegetables, 179
Roasted Garlic Potato Soup, 44, *45*
Roasted Vegetable Dip, 10, *11*
Root Veggie Soup with Curry
Croutons, 40, *41*

S
Salads
Apricot-Spinach Salad, 70, *71*
Asian Tofu Salad, 82, *83*
Black Bean Slaw with Soy-Ginger
Dressing, 92, *93*
Blue Cheese and Bean Salad, 95
Deli-Style Pasta Salad, 81
Egg Salad–Stuffed Tomatoes, 72, *73*
Fontina and Melon Salad, 69
Greek Garbanzo Salad, 90, *91*
Layered Southwestern Salad with
Tortilla Strips, 76, *77*
Mesclun Salad with Roasted Pears
and Walnuts, *67*, 68
Mexican Fiesta Salad, 78, *79*
Roasted Vegetables over Salad
Greens, 74
Salsa, Black Bean, and Rice Salad, 94
Tabbouleh with Edamame and
Feta, 86, *87*
Tarragon Bean Salad, 89
Thai Bulgur Salad, 84, *85*
Three-Bread Salad, 75
Tortellini-Vegetable Salad, 80
Wheat Berry Salad, 88
Salsa, Bean, and Cheese Pizza, 128, *129*
Salsa, Black Bean, and Rice Salad, 94
Sandwiches. *See also* **Burgers**
Artichoke and Basil Hero, 104, *105*
Eggplant Panini, 110, *111*
Egg and Vegetable Salad Wraps, 123
Ginger Tofu Salad Wraps, 121
Grilled Egg Sandwich, 150
Grilled Vegetables on Focaccia, 114

Grilled Veggie-Cheese
Sandwiches, 98, *99*
Italian Veggie Burger Bites, 120
Open-Face Ratatouille
Sandwich, 100, *101*
Pepper Stromzoni, 103
Peppery Artichoke Pitas, 106, *107*
Sautéed Onion and Tomato
Sandwiches, 102
Spinach-Mushroom
Quesadillas, 112, *113*
Spinach Panini, *97*, 109
Tofu Pitas with Mango Salsa, 108
White Bean and Goat Cheese
Wraps, 122
Sautéed Onion and Tomato
Sandwiches, 102
Savory Bean and Spinach Soup, 49
Savory Stuffed Portobellos, 227
Scalloped Potatoes and Beans, 233
Skillet Vegetables on Cheese Toast, 136
Soba-Vegetable Toss, 202, *203*
Soups. *See also* **Chili; Stews**
A to Z Vegetable Soup, 38, *39*
Bean and Potato Chowder, 58, *59*
Butternut Squash Soup with
Ravioli, 46, *47*
Caramelized Onion Soup, *37*, 43
Cheesy Mexican-Style Vegetable
Soup, 42
Cheesy Potato and Cauliflower
Chowder, 60, *61*
Greek Minestrone with Feta, 50, *51*
Jalapeño Corn Chowder, 62
Mushroom, Noodle, and Tofu
Soup, 48
Roasted Garlic Potato Soup, 44, *45*
Root Veggie Soup with Curry
Croutons, 40, *41*
Savory Bean and Spinach Soup, 49
Southwestern Bean and Cheese
Bake, 132, *133*
Spaghetti Squash with Chunky Tomato
Sauce, 230, *231*
Spicy Black Beans and Rice, 155
Spicy Tofu Triangles, 26, *27*

Spinach
    Apricot-Spinach Salad, 70, *71*
    Brown Rice–Spinach
        Custards, 174, *175*
    Poached Eggs with Grainy Mustard
        Vinaigrette, 144, *145*
    Ravioli with Spinach Pesto, 190, *191*
    Savory Bean and Spinach Soup, 49
    Spinach and Cheese Roll-Ups, 189
    Spinach and Feta Casserole, 222, *223*
    Spinach-Mushroom
        Quesadillas, 112, *113*
    Spinach Panini, *97*, 109
Spring Crustless Quiche, 146, *147*
Spring Pea Risotto, 221
Squash. *See also* **Zucchini**
    Butternut Squash Soup with
        Ravioli, 46, *47*
    Provençal Vegetable Stew, 63
    Pumpkin, Chickpea, and Red
        Lentil Stew, 64
    Ravioli with Spinach Pesto, 190, *191*
    Spaghetti Squash with Chunky
        Tomato Sauce, 230, *231*
Stews
    Black Bean and Brown Rice Stew, 65
    Provençal Vegetable Stew, 63
    Pumpkin, Chickpea, and Red Lentil
        Stew, 64
    Vegetarian Gumbo, 56, *57*
Sweet and Sour Cabbage Rolls, 232
Swiss and Olive Galette, 20, *21*

T

Tabbouleh with Edamame and
    Feta, 86, *87*
Tarragon Bean Salad, 89
Tarts
    Swiss and Olive Galette, 20, *21*
    Tomato-Zucchini Tart, 212, *213*
Tea, Apricot Iced, 32, *33*
Tex-Mex Beans with Cornmeal
    Dumplings, 164, *165*
Thai Bulgur Salad, 84, *85*
Three-Bread Salad, 75

Tofu
    Asian Tofu Salad, 82, *83*
    Baked Stuffed Shells, 206
    Cheesy Multigrain Spaghetti
        Casserole, 196, *197*
    Ginger Tofu Salad Wraps, 121
    Mushroom, Noodle, and Tofu
        Soup, 48
    Spicy Tofu Triangles, 26, *27*
    Tofruity Sipper, 31
    Tofu and Eggplant, 218, *219*
    Tofu Pitas with Mango Salsa, 108
    Udon Noodles with Tofu, 204, *205*
Tomatoes
    Avocado Pesto–Stuffed Tomatoes, 8
    Beans, Barley, and Tomatoes, 161
    Egg Salad–Stuffed Tomatoes, 72, *73*
    Grilled Veggie-Cheese
        Sandwiches, 98, *99*
    Marinara Sauce with Pasta, 195
    Oven-Roasted Vegetable Penne, 194
    Sautéed Onion and Tomato
        Sandwiches, 102
    Spaghetti Squash with Chunky
        Tomato Sauce, 230, *231*
    Tomato-Basil Rigatoni, 192, *193*
    Tomato-Zucchini Tart, 212, *213*
Tortellini Stir-Fry, 198, *199*
Tortellini-Vegetable Salad, 80
Tortillas
    Bean Burritos, 162, *163*
    Easy Cheesy Quesadillas with
        Avocado, Spinach, and
        Pepper, 130
    Egg and Vegetable Salad Wraps, 123
    Layered Southwestern Salad with
        Tortilla Strips, 76, *77*
    Mushroom-Vegetable
        Fajitas, 224, *225*
    Salsa, Bean, and Cheese
        Pizza, 128, *129*
    Spinach-Mushroom
        Quesadillas, 112, *113*
    Triple-Pepper Nachos, 28, *29*

    White Bean and Goat Cheese
        Wraps, 122
    Zesty Vegetable Enchiladas, *209*, 214
Triple-Pepper Nachos, 28, *29*

U

Udon Noodles with Tofu, 204, *205*

V

Vegetables. *See also specific vegetables*
    A to Z Vegetable Soup, 38, *39*
    Cheesy Mexican-Style Vegetable
        Soup, 42
    Easy Pasta Primavera, 201
    Fettuccine and Vegetables
        Alfredo, 200
    Fried Rice, 168, *169*
    Harvest Chili, 55
    Roasted Vegetables over Salad
        Greens, 74
    Root Veggie Soup with Curry
        Croutons, 40, *41*
    Skillet Vegetables on Cheese
        Toast, 136
    Tortellini Stir-Fry, 198, *199*
    Vegetable Casserole with Barley and
        Bulgur, 215
    Vegetable Chili with Cheese
        Topping, 54
    Vegetable Curry, 216, *217*
    Vegetable Two-Grain
        Casserole, 176, *177*
    Vegetarian Gumbo, 56, *57*
Vegetarian Gumbo, 56, *57*

W

Walnuts
    Mesclun Salad with Roasted Pears
        and Walnuts, *67*, 68
    Walnut-Cheese Risotto, 131
Wheat berries
    Multigrain Pilaf, 178
    Wheat Berry Salad, 88

White beans
Bean and Potato Chowder, 58, *59*
Blue Cheese and Bean Salad, 95
Greek Minestrone with Feta, 50, *51*
Meatless Shepherd's Pie, 160
Savory Bean and Spinach Soup, 49
White Bean and Cumin Chili, 52, *53*
White Bean and Goat Cheese
    Wraps, 122

Z

Zesty Vegetable Enchiladas, *209,* 214
Zucchini
Brown Rice Primavera, 173
Bumper-Crop Zucchini
    Pancakes, 210, *211*
Grilled Vegetables on Focaccia, 114

Open-Face Ratatouille
    Sandwich, 100, *101*
Oven-Roasted Vegetable Penne, 194
Tomato-Zucchini Tart, 212, *213*
Zesty Vegetable Enchiladas, *209,* 214
Zucchini-Carrot Burgers, 116, *117*